Effective Delegation

Better Business Guides

Getting to YES
Roger Fisher and William Ury

Janner's Complete Letterwriter
Greville Janner QC, MP

The Telephone Marketing Book
Pauline Marks

The Basic Arts of Financial Management
Third edition
Leon Simons

The Basic Arts of Marketing
Second edition
Ray L. Willsmer

Effective Delegation

Clive T. Goodworth

Business Books

London   Melbourne   Sydney   Auckland   Johannesburg

Business Books Ltd
An imprint of the Hutchinson Publishing Group
62–65 Chandos Place, London WC2N 4NW

Hutchinson Publishing Group (Australia) Pty Ltd
16–22 Church Street, Hawthorn, Melbourne, Victoria 3122

Hutchinson Group (NZ) Ltd
32–34 View Road, PO Box 40-086, Glenfield, Auckland 10

Hutchinson Group (SA) (Pty) Ltd
PO Box 337, Bergvlei 2012, South Africa

Brookfield Publishing Company, Inc.
Old Post Road, Brookfield, Vermont 05036 USA

First published 1985
© Clive T. Goodworth, 1985

Set in Palatino by Folio Photosetting, Bristol

Made and printed in Great Britain by the
Guernsey Press Co. Ltd., Guernsey, Channel Islands.

British Library Cataloguing in Publication Data

Goodworth, Clive T.
    Effective delegation.
    1   Delegation of authority
    I   Title
    658.4'02   HD50

ISBN 0 09 161780 4 (cased)
       0 09 161781 2 (paper)

Dedicated with loving affection to my father,
Ronald William Goodworth. Thanks, Dad

Contents

Introduction

When I gives yer th'word o'command, yer don't fink abaht nuffink, yer leaps inter friggin' action – RIGHT?

When, long ago, a ten-feet-tall drill sergeant thus whispered in my square-bashing ear, I distinctly recall that as I leapt into friggin' action, I did have the audacity to fink – and, probably for the first time in my life, thought about delegation. Today, countless moons and management scars later, I still think about it – and, reader, cramming one theme of this book into the proverbial nutshell, it mightn't be such a bad idea if you did too. But hold on a tick. . . . My publisher (on whom may the sun never set) has quite rightly suggested that I should provide something more than a measly, truncated hint of my intentions – so here goes.

For openers, let me toss at you the indisputable fact that far too many executives tend to take delegation for granted. Or, to put it another way, individual managers seldom get round to questioning their personal proficiency in the art – which is faintly ironic when one considers just how readily we all criticize that self-same ability in others. Piling on the agony, only a miniscule number of bosses ever recognize that this interminable handing-down of jobs is not only a complex process – but, also and sadly, comprises an activity in which pitfalls abound. In short, we skate gaily over the surface of management's thinnest and most dangerous ice – and then, when disaster strikes, bleat like fury at finding ourselves up to the top-knot in the shark-ridden waters of failure.

There, if you like, are some of the reasons why I've decided to write a book on delegation. We'll kick off by taking a look at the manner in which the process has stuck with management over the centuries – and follow this basic, scene-setting stuff with a hefty chunk or two on what I choose to call delegation warts. With the latter section in mind, it could be a pity that my publisher has rejected my suggestion that the book should be supplied with a free tin hat – for there's bound to be some shrapnel flying about.

Since I've no wish to make this introduction a mere carbon copy of the contents list, suffice it to say that, one way or another, my aim is to proceed from delegation warts on a measured but hard-hitting romp through all the other, equally important aspects of the process. One thing is certain, while it's my intention to set the stage with a fair old number of scenarios, the thought behind them will remain rock-constant: *the only way by which managers can hope to survive the rat-race, let alone concentrate on their primary responsibilities, is by practising effective delegation.*

However, a word of caution to the unwary. . . . The reader who expects to be presented with an erudite, jargon-stuffed exposition on delegation is in for a big disappointment – because, quite simply, being a run-of-the-mill, sharp-end guy, I hate such deathly-boring textbooks. Similarly, the reader who wishes to be transported on a bump-free glissade through pages of anaesthetic gobbledegook will also suffer – for, in addition to umpteen potholes, there are several minefields on the road ahead. Ah, yes, and I give my personal guarantee that if anyone's going to do any work throughout our association, it's not going to be me – and, reader, you'd better believe it!

1 Brass tacks

For this real or imagined overwork there are, broadly speaking, three possible remedies. He (A) may resign; he may ask to halve the work with a colleague called B; he may demand the assistance of two subordinates, to be called C and D. There is probably no instance in history, however, of A choosing any but the third alternative.

C. Northcote Parkinson
Parkinson's Law

Think in terms of delegation – and, however irrelevant it may seem, consider in the same mental breath the legendary Step Pyramid, built at Saqqara, Egypt, by the architect Imhotep in the thirtieth century BC. It will never be known whether Imhotep's foremost aim was the utter grandeur of this monument to Pharoah Zozer, or simply the tactical employment of discontented villagers during the regular Nile inundations. However, one thing is certain; the project entailed the quarrying, transport and erection of some 600 000 tons of stone – an operation of mind-boggling complexity, which depended for its ultimate success on the large-scale organization of literally thousands of workers. Moving forward in time, it was around 1360 BC that a wily young king named Amenhotep IV became disillusioned with his unruly subjects and, determined to make them pay for their sins, founded Egypt's first civil service. The obvious point is, there can be little doubt that both Imhotep and Amenhotep, to quote but two examples from the annals of ancient history, were entirely familiar with delegation.

Plainly, the process by which those in control allocate work to their subordinates has been an integral feature of management throughout the ages. Unfortunately, as most of us would admit, the state of the art has not vastly improved over the centuries – and, in these competitive days, this continuing propensity for poor delegation can, and often does, land far too many managers in inescapably hot water. The three-fold aim of this book is to examine the process in all its varied aspects, offer plenty of food for thought on the subject – and, last but certainly not least, provide practical hints and tips on how you, reader, may best grapple with the beast. Hullo, and welcome!

To begin with, I would like to seek your views on something which, to me, is quite mystifying. Let me explain it this way. When next you visit the public library, just pluck from the shelves any textbook on general management techniques that happens to strike your eye – and, making quick use of the index, turn up the author's offering on delegation. The odds are that you will find yourself gazing at little more than a few, sparsely detailed paragraphs on the subject; or, if you are really unlucky, at a mere five or six lines of superlatively unrewarding information. Now, I appreciate that this smacks of a rude dig at the writer-gurus of the management world, but hold on – does it not pose a sixty-thousand-dollar question? Is it right and proper that one of the potentially most effective and, all too often, most damaging functions of management should be dismissed in such cavalier fashion? For this man's money, it is not. If this book has an underlying theme, it just has to be: *delegation is an explosive subject – handle like eggs*.

Pressing the message home, whatever your executive or other niche in working life, look upon delegation in much the same way as you may well regard nuclear fission; namely, as a latent boon offering untold opportunities for success – but also as something which, given the slightest mishandling, can blow you to management perdition. And, again, that is what this book is all about.

Kicking off from square one

I make no apology at all for launching our extensive foray with a very basic, dictionary-type definition:

delegate (*noun*)   A person appointed by another, with power to act on his or her behalf, or transact business as a duly authorized representative; a deputy.

(*verb*)   To commit or entrust; to depute; to appoint as a representative, with authority to act.

Having thus set the stage with minimal props, it is necessary to take a second look at history – not, I hasten to add, at the management practices of the ancient Egyptians, but at more recent and relevant times. If you are at all familiar with the make-up of basic courses in general management, you'll likely know that, early on in most such programmes, some lecturer or other will launch into an exposition on 'management styles'. More to the point, the speaker will refer with considerable relish to one style in particular, *autocratic management* – which, because it appeared to work eminently well, was practised from feudal times until well into the Industrial Revolution (and, as some unfortunates know to their cost, is still so practised by the odd, Machiavellian employer). How, then, did the process of delegation fare during this long period of management by autocracy?

In order to obtain a near-objective answer, it is advisable to take more than a tunnel-visioned peep at what went on. Certainly, the many contemporary accounts of agricultural slavery and dark satanic mills of the Industrial Revolution are salutary lessons in truth, but not the whole truth. Contrary to what is popularly supposed, for many who possessed the proverbial fire in the belly, the period was a time for self-help and optimism – in that numbers of poverty-stricken workers rose from the lowliest rungs of the ladder to become factory owners and veritable captains of industry. More to the point, it is necessary to gain an accurate appreciation of the management philosophy of the period, which was simple and direct. God had gazed on the British people and, liking what he saw, had endowed them with a natural energy-cum-ability second to none. Since the works of the Almighty brooked absolutely no interference, it followed that any move to change the workers' lot would be playing straight into the hands of the Devil. Consequently, working terms and conditions were deliberately maintained at what we now know to be extremely harsh levels; but, of course, were never regarded by the bosses in that light – for, in their eyes, such things were part-and-parcel of the divine ordinance. Not surprisingly, the attitude of these God-fearing employers to the whole process of allocating tasks and duties to subordinates was equally misguided – to the extent that, had a management author of the period (and there's a curiosity, indeed) thought of writing about delegation, he might well have urged along the following lines:

> Delegation, the means by which a Master shall achieve the fruition of that which he demands of his servant, relies for its essential vitality upon the degree to which he seeks and obtains Unquestioning Obedience. In order that he shall attain this laudable end, a Master should strive to implement each of several disciplines, his observance in the matter being diligent and scrupulous withal.

1   A Master shall voice his commands in a forthright manner, as befits his station and the authority vested in him by a Divine Providence.

2   A Master's commands shall always be addressed directly to the manager or overseer, who in his turn shall pass such instruction as is necessary to his subordinates, and so on and so forth, until such time as the commands rest with those who, by their office, are destined to obey.

3   When delivering his commands, a Master shall ensure that the manager or overseer to whom they are directed is aware in every particular that, as the Master's appointed and privileged deputy, he bears irrevocable and absolute responsibility for the effective discharge of the duties thus imposed.

4   A Master shall also ensure that the clarity and import of his commands are not sullied by his permitting the intrusion of conversation or debate; for the role of the servant is, and ever shall be, to obey his Master without question.

5   A Master shall never allow this process of delegation to provide any implied or actual opportunity for a worker to rise beyond his allotted station; for it is as a result of such personal weakness that a Master

shall encourage false pride and disruptive ambition in his servant, the which being an offence against the Holy Writ.

6   If ever it transpires, which God in his wisdom forbid, that a Master's commands are not executed in swift or proper manner, it is his bounden duty to impose stern punishment on those who have thus earned his retribution. It should ever be remembered that such fundamental breaches of faith are without defence, and summary discharge from employment must invariably ensue.

7   A Master shall never express his faith in the ability of a servant to perform as he is from time to time commanded so to do; for it is implicit in the employment of the servant that he shall perform ably and well throughout his service, and such comment is therefore superfluous. A perspicacious Master will also understand that, for the self-same reason, it is not wise and in no manner necessary to make laudatory observation on the successful completion of that which he has commanded; for undue praise seeds arrogance in those of lowly station.

So, there we have it, the process of delegation as viewed by those who, priding themselves on their rectitude, wielded the mighty big stick of autocratic management. Of course, it could be said that one excuse for this long-lived state of affairs is the fact that it was not until the advent of the twentieth century that management *per se* became a subject for research and comment. Be that as it may, those early concepts of delegation were pretty dreadful:

>   DO IT
>   DO IT MY WAY
>   DON'T EXPECT ANY THANKS
>   JUST DO IT . . .

As every student of management should know (simply because it is an essential part of his catechism), it was in 1916 that Henri Fayol, a French industrialist and gifted management thinker, compiled what are now generally regarded as the first 'principles of management' – and, in so doing, threw a healthy pinch of leavening into the delegation mix:

>   'The manager who desires loyalty and devotion in his workers will treat them with kindliness and justice.'

Treat employees with kindliness and justice? This was great stuff, indeed. From that long overdue start, albeit encouraged by hefty prods from an increasingly emancipated working population, management's attitude to delegation over the intervening years has certainly shown some improvement – but, in case we forget the message, not nearly enough.

Pursuing this introductory, ice-breaking theme, let us focus our attention

16

APROPOS OF SOMETHING No. 1

Our management past is chock-a-block with examples of egotistical and untrustworthy characters who, when they were literally forced to delegate, stamped the process with artifice and unyielding autocracy. One such scallywag was His Majesty Charles I, who could not have started his reign more badly when, in 1625, he continued to delegate powers to his favourite, the villainous Duke of Buckingham – the most hated man in England. Then, would you believe, in 1628 (having delegated authority to Parliament by reluctantly agreeing to the Petition of Right, which restated many of the terms of Magna Carta), he whizzed back on his word, dissolved Parliament in a trice – and, true to form, reigned as a dictator for the next eleven years. During this period he attempted to swell his dwindling coffers by means of various delegation chicaneries, including the appointment of an army of worthies as tax collectors and fund-raisers – all of them wielding highly dubious and oft-illegal authority. When, by 1640, all this skulduggery had failed to produce sufficient filthy lucre, Charles had to recall Parliament – but this time, the Members stood firm, and the moment had arrived for the Royalists and Roundheads to have their civil set-to. It was in January 1649 that greed, stubborn arrogance and stinking delegation finally cost Chas Stuart his head.

on the present; and, in particular, on the manner in which the delegation process impinges on the very fabric of business and industrial life – to wit, *the working organization*.

Be upstanding for the company hierarchy

Anyone who owns shares will be acutely aware that, despite all the legal huzz-buzz about the shareholders being the owners of a company, he stands precious little chance of having any real say in the day-to-day running of his chosen investment. Owing entirely to the Great God Apathy, whose opiate runs like treacle in the veins of the average investor, it is virtually impossible for any man-in-the-street shareholder, however keen he may be on wielding some influence, to muster the vital support of his fellows. Nearly every company secretary who faces the task of arranging an Annual General Meeting pays obeisance to the said god – happy in the knowledge that he need only hire a moderately sized room and lay in a few turkey sandwiches to provide for the miniscule number of shareholders who'll actually attend the event.

But, for all this, a public limited company is held in stewardship by its management, and the shareholders are the rightful owners – it's just a sad fact of life that pretty well all of their powers are (aye, clever-clogs, you've got it in one) DELEGATED. True, the transfer of authority only hops down one tiny step in the hierarchy; but, so far as the investors are concerned, it might just as well be outer space – for that simple little act places the ball well and truly at the feet of the board of directors, who'll move heaven and earth to prevent it passing back. Apropos of all this, does the following quote by a real-life director happen to ring any bells?

> 'Shareholders – well, what about 'em? They're a damned nuisance at the best of times. . . . Feed 'em an annual glossy with bags of flannel about management's heroics in the face of recession – oh, yes, and hold the AGM in the Orkneys, that's what I say.'

A management equivalent of the Rosetta Stone (and there may well be one tucked away somewhere) would probably remind us that a board of directors has special responsibilities for all that they dictate towards the shareholders, customers, employees and, would you believe, the community at large. Headed by a chairman, who will have graduated to the seat of power by way of coercion, divine right or even a democratic vote, the directing board will often comprise an ad-mix of:

Executive directors   Full-time employees who, because they are enmeshed in the day-to-day running of specialist aspects of the company's operations, may well have partisan views when they enter the boardroom. An executive director may also be painfully aware that he is required to live with his managing director and his colleagues outside the boardroom – and we all know what that can mean.

Non-executive directors   The official party line on the merits of acquiring these part-time and, hence, more independent members of the board is usually that they bring to bear external, specialist expertise – which, of course, can only be good for the outfit concerned. However, since far too many companies are up to their corporate gunnels in organization vanity, it very often happens that Charles Frederick Blenkinsop, MP, or Lady So-and-So is hired purely for his or her decorative value – sublimely regardless of the fact that the person concerned is a bumbling idiot of the first degree.

Be all that as it may, the board of directors carry out their delegated role of deciding policy – and, in their turn, delegate the task of carrying out that policy to the managing director. Ideally, this most senior member of full-time management, rightly styled the chief executive and focal point of the organization, should squat in his rosewood-lined boudoir rather after the fashion of a queen bee; wholly absorbed in the laying of plans and strategies for the future, and in the motivation of his senior management team – to whom he has *delegated* almost the entire day-to-day task of successfully running the outfit. However, since the managing director (despite many indications to the contrary) is human, he often tends to succumb to that very human weakness of plonking his finger in his subordinates' personal pies. His position of virtual isolation in the hierarchy, coupled with the fact that, if they can get away with it, the management will only feed him with what they wish him to know, is a powerful spur to such meddling – but more of this anon. Suffice it to say that, if the *continuing process of delegation* downwards in the average hierarchy was carried out with even near-success, there would be little justification for this book. *But it isn't, and there is . . .*

I suggest we round off this part of our back-to-basics chapter with the reminder that, if any organization is to function efficiently, the delegation catchword must be *'ever-downwards'*. The continual round of passing out tasks to subordinates does not and must not come to a grinding halt until little Willie, the smallest and most insignificant coglet in the outfit, has received his rightful share.

But delegation – unlike water – can also flow uphill

Fortunately, while some would attempt to devalue and undermine its importance, the principle (if not always the application) of democracy remains a salient feature of our general way of life, and is certainly not without significance in the world of work. Just as Emily Blenkinsop attains by democratic process a much-coveted seat on the Parish Council, and, albeit with a selection of reservations, some political party or other succeeds by franchise to the tenancy of government – so, too, do many works committee representatives, shop stewards and trade union national executives use elections to gain their respective positions. It is worth remembering that, in all such work-related set-ups, the democratic intention (again, if not the practice) is that the winning majority authorizes and instructs those duly elected to represent its interests – by delegation *upwards*. This does not, or should not, signify that an electorate is subordinate to those it elects, but merely that the delegation flow is in reverse to that more commonly encountered in business and industry. As I've intimated, it's worth bearing in mind.

Self-tutorial

The aim of this scene-setting chapter is to get you thinking about delegation in general – and, like it or not, the next few pages are designed to probe and test that preliminary thought. So, reader, it's now time to nip away and dig out pencil and paper – and, yes, while you're about it, it mightn't be such a bad idea to put the kettle on.

Since I'm being quite open with my crafty intention that you're the one who's going to do all the work, it shouldn't come as too much of a surprise to find one of these 'self-tutorials' tacked on the end of each chapter. Their purpose is two-fold; firstly, to provide you with a facility for recapping and expanding this and that piece of information by means of various exercises, many of an investigative nature – and secondly, to occasionally throw you in at the deep end with stuff we haven't even touched, let alone explored. If you'll pardon my donning the teacher's mortar-board for a second; having bought, borrowed or simply pinched this book, it's plainly in your interests to extract as much value as you can from its pages – ergo, eyes down and get cracking!

Come to think of it, this first self-tutorial is a fairly gentle one; and, laying on the balm thick and fast, you'll even find a few answer-clues at the end. Now, being a hard-working, honourable reader, you wouldn't dream of cheating, would you?

A mini-quiz to set you in the mood

Go on, be a devil – they're very simple questions. Just have a shot at filling in the blanks:

1 ...... is the assignment of authority and responsibility to another person for the purpose of carrying out specified activities.

2 It is a generally recognized principle of management that responsibility for specified tasks should be delegated to the ...... level in an organization at which the employees concerned possess sufficient ability and information to carry them out exactly as required.

3 Following on from Question 2, this means that, if delegation is carried out on a correct scale, ... employees will be afforded adequate opportunities to exercise their skills and experience.

4 When a manager assigns responsibility to a subordinate, this does not absolve him from .... for the successful completion of the task concerned.

5 In order for a subordinate to perform a delegated task effectively, he must be assigned an adequate level of ...... to enable him to carry out that task.

Well, that wasn't too bad, was it? Before you check the answer-clues and award yourself 100 per cent, plough straight on to the next chunk.

Appraising the appraiser

As a senior executive within your organization, one of your many responsibilities is to vet and countersign your managers' periodic appraisals of their subordinates. While engaged on this chore, your attention is drawn to a narrative report written by one such manager, John Winter, on the overall performance of an office supervisor named Colin Harris – and also to the section headed *Comments by person reported upon following appraisal discussion*.

- NARRATIVE SUMMARY BY REPORTING MANAGER

'During the period of this report, Mr Harris has exercised a generally efficient control over his section, and I have been impressed by the manner in which he has succeeded in motivating the ten members of staff to give of their best. Having stated thus, I feel bound to make mention of certain instances when his performance has reflected levels of professional weakness which are not only worrying, but quite unacceptable.

'The first such occasion arose as a direct result of the recent summary dismissal of a sales department employee, when the man concerned made a formal request for a detailed written statement of the reasons for his dismissal. Since Mr Harris's duties as personnel office supervisor include a responsibility for all 'non-routine' items of correspondence, he was required to prepare and issue the necessary document, and this he did. Unfortunately, it was not until I personally received a telephone call from the ex-employee's solicitor that I learned that the statement issued by Mr Harris contained two serious errors of fact – which, needless to say, created an embarrassing and difficult situation. I informed Mr Harris at the time and I now reiterate that he displayed a lamentable lack of care in his entire approach to this routine but crucially important matter.

'Sadly, barely a fortnight after this episode I again found it necessary to interview Mr Harris concerning his failure to exercise due care in the performance of his duties – this time, in relation to an event which took place immediately prior to the Christmas break. Having issued my customary reminder to him that, in the interests of road safety, there was to be no festive drinking during working hours, I was extremely perturbed to find that my instruction had been wilfully circumvented. On the last day of work, the office staff returned from their lunch-break exhibiting obvious signs of over-indulgence – and, while I stress that Mr Harris was himself a model of sobriety, it was transparently clear that he had failed to sufficiently impress his authority and the tenor of my instruction on his subordinates.

'I regard Mr Harris as a supervisor with some potential, but he must understand that if he is to progress further in his career with this company, he cannot afford such serious lapses in care and vigilance. It is my hope that he has learned his lesson, and that his future performance will justify my faith, and that of the company, in his appointment.'

J. Winter
Administration Manager

- COMMENTS BY PERSON REPORTED UPON FOLLOWING APPRAISAL DISCUSSION

'I have read the above report and wish to say that I disagree with Mr Winter's comments regarding my alleged lapses in care and attention. With regard to the errors in the dismissal statement, I accept that I made the mistakes, but I did point out to Mr Winters at the time that I was having difficulty owing to conflicting information supplied by two managers. He told me to use my best judgement, and that is what I did. As for the matter of the Christmas drinking, I did pass Mr Winter's instruction to the staff, but as I explained to him later that afternoon, I did not go to the pub with the staff because I still had some shopping to do. I do not think I can be held responsible for what staff choose to do in their spare time. Anyway, they all completed their work properly that afternoon, and nobody was the worse for wear.

'I wish to appeal against Mr Winter's report on me.'

Colin Harris
Personnel Office Supervisor

Having ploughed through Winter's summary and the unhappy supervisor's comments, you are now faced with the prospect of interviewing Harris on the subject of his grievance. On the basis of the limited information available, what would be your planned course of action? Make a few notes and place 'em on one side for a moment. I'm sorry if the coffee's getting cold, but there's a bit more to be done before we get to the answer-clues.

Another look at that downward delegation stuff

In reminding you of the manner in which delegation flows downward within an organization, Figure 1 also serves to illustrate the effect of the process on the allocation of time at various levels of management to two vitally different functions:

- Managing – the delegating function
- Operating – the 'doing' function

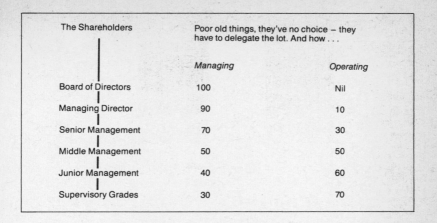

The Shareholders	Poor old things, they've no choice – they have to delegate the lot. And how . . .	
	Managing	Operating
Board of Directors	100	Nil
Managing Director	90	10
Senior Management	70	30
Middle Management	50	50
Junior Management	40	60
Supervisory Grades	30	70

Figure 1 *Percentage proportions of time spent managing (delegating) and operating ('doing') at various levels of management*

Later in these pages we shall be looking in some detail at the vexed question of 'how much' an executive should delegate – but, for the present, suffice it to say that the higher one climbs on the management ladder, the more time one should spend *managing*, and the less *operating*. The proportions, although obviously very approximate, are not without interest.

Bearing in mind that, thus far, we are merely attempting to gain a broad 'overview' of this thing called delegation (for there is a whole stack of nitty-gritty just around the corner), take a general look at your own 'managing' and 'operating' functions. Are your proportions of time spent anywhere near similar to the relevant figures in the diagram? While mulling over the point, don't waste time trying to calculate how much work you delegate to others, for it's far easier to assess the proportion of time you devote to routine 'doing' tasks during a typical day – and arrive at an approximate ratio by that avenue of approach.

Your crib-bank

And now, as a form of respite before we *really* get cracking, it's hey-ho for the answer-clues.

First, the answers to the very basic mini-quiz:

1 Delegation
2 lowest
3 all
4 ultimate responsibility (and you'd better believe it . . .)
5 authority

If, as I expect, you got them all correct, good on you. But, prith'ee, don't feel too sanguine about your success, for there is very much worse in store in later chapters!

I'm fairly confident that your initial reaction to Winter's write-up on poor old Harris was, to say the least, decisive – for, after all, reading between the lines of the summary, he really is a shocking character.

The business of the written statement of reasons for dismissal, albeit described in scant detail, betrays him as suffering from that most contagious of management ills, *delegation diarrhoea* – and his office supervisor has plainly been caught in the wretched fall-out. Having clobbered Harris with the blanket responsibility for dealing with so-called 'non-routine' correspondence, the vile creature then leaves his subordinate to cope alone and unaided with the complications (the indication is that there were complications) of compiling a near-legal document – or, more precisely, a document that could easily constitute a hair-trigger for legal action.* Implicit in the report is the *hard fact* that Winter hadn't even bothered to check the statement before despatch (one can even imagine that he left Harris to sign the thing), and this is a venal sin committed by a manager who has probably abrogated, not delegated, his responsibilities. In all the circumstances, the supervisor cannot really be blamed for much other than failing to raise an objection with Winter in the first place – and, for all we know, he might well have done exactly that, only to be told to get on with things and stop making a fuss about nothing.

As for the drinking episode – well, I ask you, who the devil does Winter think he is? If Harris tells the truth in his comments, and he did pass on the instruction to the staff, and if his observation to the effect that the afternoon's work was completed without a hiccup is also true – then Winter's case plops to the floor like a lump of wet dough. In any event and whatever the truth might be, the manager's decision to highlight the affair in his report was at best a poor one – and, at worst, manifestly unfair.

Be all that as it may, the exercise required you to decide on a planned course of action over Harris's grievance. The sting in the tail of this particular little assignment is quite simply that, whatever your reaction (including, I might add, an impatient, know-all shrug of the shoulders and outright rejection of the task as time-wasting and absurd), *it will have been cast in the mould of your personal management style*. Consequently, there is a fairly massive variety of 'possible solutions' – but here are just a few for your conscience to play with:

---

* Current UK legislation (the Employment Protection [Consolidation] Act 1978) provides that a dismissed employee may require his ex-employer to provide a detailed statement of the reasons for his dismissal – and caters for compensation through an industrial tribunal if this is not forthcoming, or if it is established to be inaccurate or untrue.

Autocratic style	'I'd sack Harris for incompetence, and kick Winter out for precisely the same reason.'
	'I haven't got time to worry about a mere supervisor's whimperings – that's Winter's baby, that's what he's paid for. . . . If he can't hack his job as admin manager, I'd get rid of him.'
Democratic style	(Remember, the democratic leader is the manager who is probably uncertain of himself and his dealings with others – he likes to go along with the majority, popular view.)
	'I'd like Winter and Harris to get together and sort their own problems out – and let me know the happy result. . . .'
Consultative/ participative style	(The manager with this commendable style of management will seek to involve others, but not at the cost of giving up control.)
	'I'd interview both Winter and Harris at some length, with the object of more fully establishing the facts – and base my course of action on the outcome.'

So, when ploughing through the following chapters, never forget that it's not just a case of improving your delegation techniques – of simply learning a certain drill off pat. *It could and may well be that you will have to give some solid thought to the question of your management style.*

And that, friend, is a totally different ball-game.

2 Some delegation warts

To him, delegating work is rather like donating blood –
frightening to contemplate, messy in the giving and, worst of all,
entailing a personal and irreplaceable loss.

Extract from a manager-student's project
on Effective Delegation

When senior managers get together to talk about, among many other things,
their subordinates (and, life being what it is, when all subordinates get
together to chew over the sole topic of their seniors), it's a pretty fair bet that,
early on in such glorious chinwags, someone or other will utter those
immortal words:

'Of course, the trouble is, she doesn't delegate enough. . . .'

Sometimes the sentiment is expressed in slightly stronger terms:

'If only the ignorant so-and-so would delegate. . . .'

If, as I hope you will agree, delegation is the very process on which the work
of an organization depends (for why else have one?), it would seem that any
reference at all to *under*-delegation, let alone a whole chapter, is superfluous,
if not utterly senseless. Huh, would that it were. . . . The stark, glaring truth of
the matter is that a whole legion of managers appear to be constitutionally
incapable of handing out work to their subordinates in fair and challenging
chunks – and, since I'm not one to wrap up my words in cosy niceties, the
purpose of this chapter is to trigger you, reader, into discovering whether or
not you're a regular soldier in this particular bunch of ne'er-do-wells.

There is only one way to establish the degree, if any, of your infection. So,
without further ado, let us take a candidly close look at the several and nasty
reasons why so many executives do under-delegate; and, as an inevitable
consequence, contrive to place their self-respect, the esteem of others, and
their very jobs firmly on the line.

Management lethargy

I know – and I'm jolly certain you know – that lethargy or downright
laziness, call it what you like, is a virulent bug that runs freely in the veins of
managers the world over. But how many of those so afflicted will confess

their indolence? It would be very easy for me to merely remind you of the obvious; that management lethargy is a root cause of under-delegation – and, like so many others in this textbook-writing game, just leave it at that. If, and I only say if, you *are* guilty as charged, that kind of homily would just bounce off your thick hide with nary a trace of effect. Again, if we're honest, we both know that one outstanding corollary of laziness is an almost in-built ability for the person so affected to practise self-deception, to cosily exercise the mind with such sterling thoughts as:

'I'm not REALLY lazy – I just like to get my priorities right. . . .'

'It's not worth working myself to death for the piddling amount they pay me.'

'It's not my fault that I hate the job. . . .'

So, in view of this innate yen of the work-shy to kid themselves, stick with me while we eavesdrop on a senior executive who just happens to be talking to a colleague about a certain manager . . .

'. . . the thing that surprises me about young Jefferson is the fact that he's quite certain no one has twigged his little game – after all, he's not without intelligence, and I for one would expect a bit more expertise from a guy like him when it comes to acting out a part. . . . I've been watching him closely of late – and the fact is, he's bone idle. Oh, yes, he makes a big song and dance about always having bags of work to do – the piled-up desk, the look of intense concentration when he thinks anyone's observing him, and so on. . . . And, of course, there's one aspect of his laziness that sticks out like a sore thumb, and that's his utter failure to get his staff cracking work-wise. Y'know how the word gets round. Mary, my secretary, hears more moans and niggles from his group than any other section in the headquarters. . . . But one doesn't have to listen to gossip to know what's going on. The section's efficiency has got steadily worse over the last couple of months – and with half of 'em sitting around waiting to be told what to do it's easy to understand why.... Anyway, I'm having the blighter in this afternoon. I'm going to give him his marching-orders, and good riddance, too....'

To which her colleague responds:

'Well, Joyce, he's your man and, strictly speaking, it's none of my business – but I'm not surprised that you're going to give him the kick.... As you know, we don't have much to do with Costing on our side of the house – but, for all that, even I've heard that Jefferson's got himself a name for sitting on his fanny and doing damn-all, especially where his staff are concerned. It's the old, old story – failure to delegate.... I reckon it's as you say, good riddance to bad rubbish, eh?'

All right, that is a blatantly obvious illustration – but then, the vast majority of lethargic, lazy types are obvious to all who witness their indolence. Sadly, the reason why so many of them remain in their posts is because their bosses are either apathetic or just plain management cowards.

But, so far as you are concerned, reader, isn't all this business about failure to delegate through lethargy completely academic? I have no doubt at all that you regard yourself as a hard-working manager who delegates fairly and squarely whenever necessary – so there's only one question I'd like to pose: *Would your subordinates agree?*

Concern for prestige

There are very few managers who, in their heart of hearts, regard personal prestige as an unimportant factor in their executive lives. This is hardly surprising, for the urge to win the various trappings which, in sum, represent 'status' in the eyes of others is a powerful human motivator – and one which most thinking employers will do much to exploit. How do you view the question of personal prestige at work? Would you go along with the following opinion?

'The importance of prestige in one's job? Well, I reckon it's very important – at least, if I'm honest, it's important to me.... As you know, I got my first really decent promotion last year, when they made me works manager.... All right, I didn't get a massive increase in salary –but I did get my very first company car. Believe you me, that means something, and not only in money terms.... It's – well, it's a kind of confirmation, if you like, that I've arrived, that I'm well and truly on the ladder. Also, I've got a much better office, and a secretary as well. That all adds up to my having a good deal more prestige than I've ever had before – and, yes, I think it's important.... After all, it's an incentive, isn't it?
(Some nicely frank observations by a manager during a seminar discussion on management development.)

Nicely, but not totally frank.... It took another, more perceptive member of the group to cap this manager's comments with a notable rider:

'I go along with everything you've said – but what about the factor of work itself? In my opinion, where prestige is concerned, the job one's given to do is just as important as all the perks. . . .'

There is no doubt that this latter chappie had a point. The levels of responsibility and authority inherent in any job are public and very cogent indicators of the incumbent's status – *and, in delegation terms, can trigger some mighty snags*. The manager who shows an excessive and unhealthy concern for supposed loss of prestige will almost invariably hang on like grim death to every slightest duty or particle of work that crops up – and heaven help the poor, delegation-starved subordinates.

It's worth repeating the question: *How do YOU view personal prestige at work?*

Fear of being superseded

At a time when the world of work seems fated to reel under a never-ending cycle of recession and redundancy, only the super-confident (or super-lucky?) can lay truthful claim to freedom from anxiety. In countries throughout the Western world, even those classic exponents of job security, civil servants, are increasingly under attack by the twin ogres of so-called 'rationalization' and staff economies – but tragically, the manager whose hopes for a secure livelihood are pinned on the vagaries of commercial or industrial employment is far more at risk. Accepting that, with things as they currently are, there is good reason for most of us to be assailed with doubts and uncertainty over our jobs, just think what it must be like for the 'professional worriers' in our midst. . . .

Yes, this fear of being superseded, of being thrown on the scrap-heap, mounts to an all-time high when the economic situation goes haywire – but, even when everything in the employment garden is lovely, the professional worrier will still be racked with countless, oft-intangible and illogical anxieties. You really don't need me to remind you that the one hallowed way for Jack or Jill to avoid being dispensed with is, of course, to become indispensable. . . . To the nervously insecure executive, desperately trying to dodge a real or imagined quick bullet, this means a frantic, never-ending round of work at anything and everything – and, more often than not, all at the cost of gross under-delegation.

Exactly how often is *your* head over your shoulder at work?

Lack of confidence in one's subordinates

Of all the multifarious ills, plain lack of confidence in one's subordinates is probably the most common and certainly the most virulent complaint to which executives are prone. Let's take a look at the various lines of defence put forward by the manager who professes to be saddled with such ill-supportive members of staff:

'They're just not interested in doing a good job. . . .'

'He's plain incompetent . . .'

'With the time it takes to get through their thick heads what needs to be done, it's far quicker AND easier to do it myself. . . .'

'Once my back's turned, they're up to all kinds of tricks. . . .'

And so on, *ad infinitum.*

While we are primarily concerned with the manner in which this lack of confidence affects the delegation process, I would like to pop off on a worth-while tangent – and pose the following questions for your candid consideration:

- Who is responsible for provoking and maintaining the interest of subordinates in their work?

- Who is responsible for ensuring that they're fully competent at what they do?

- Who is at fault when it takes an unduly long time for them to understand and appreciate instructions?

- Whose duty is it to maintain good order and discipline at all times?

    WELL NOW, COULD IT JUST BE – YOU?

To resume, it matters little whether this particular delegation weakness is founded in solid fact or, as is too often the case, in pure figments of the imagination. In either event, the executive thus infected is guilty, not only of under-delegation, but of dire mismanagement as well.

A consuming interest in doing the job

They may be a bit thin on the ground in your territory, but there are numbers of them around – those workaholic-type managers who have such an all-abiding interest in their labour that, try as they might, they cannot let a single shred of it be delegated to others. While it is fair to say that some managers are genuinely and quite unfairly overloaded with work, it remains a fact that, of all those characters who (to quote but one example) bear bulging briefcases home day after day, a goodly percentage are folk who have selfishly refused to delegate realistically and well.

31

Having thus reminded you of five root causes of under-delegation, it is now necessary that we proceed to the intensely personal business of establishing whether you, reader, are happily free from this particular brand of infection. It is my hope that this will not prove to be too bumpy a ride. . . .

A questionnaire

Needless to say, the efficacy of this and all the other questionnaires in the pages that follow depends entirely on the candour of your responses. I am sure you will wish to extract full value from our joint, in-depth look at the delegation process – and to this end I can do no better than commend to your attention William Shakespeare's sterling words:

> This above all: to thine own self be true,
> And it must follow, as the night the day,
> Thou canst not then be false to any man.

Apropos of nothing, if a manager was looking for a golden rule with which to enlighten his executive life, is that not it?

The following questions are wholly concerned with the people who are within your *direct* span of control (i.e. the person[s] positioned in the 'first layer' immediately beneath you in your organization hierarchy) – NOT all the others who happen to be junior to your position, but who are directly controlled by your subordinate(s). Putting it another way, we are concerned at present with *your* approach to delegation, not that of your subordinates.

Having studied each question, select the most appropriate answer from those provided – and, if you wish to avoid marking these pristine pages, make a note of your selections on a separate piece of paper. You will need to refer to them later on.

1 How confident are you that you do not under-delegate?
   a   Very confident.
   b   Fairly confident.
   c   I'm afraid I am prone to under-delegation.
   d   I consistently under-delegate.   (   )

2 When did you last discuss 'delegation loads' with your subordinates?
   a   Certainly within the last six months.
   b   I can't remember exactly when, but I'm fairly sure I have done so at some time or other.
   c   As a specific topic, never – but I think the subject has come up in general conversation.
   d   To my knowledge, never.   (   )

3 Are you required to complete a periodic formal appraisal report on your subordinate(s)?
   a   No.
   b   Yes.   (   )

4 Honestly, now, harking back to that business of the time spent by different executive grades on 'managing' and 'operating' functions (Figure 1), how did you assess your personal ratio?
   a   Very close to the appropriate percentages listed in Figure 1 for 'my' grade.
   b   Using Figure 1 as a yardstick, I spend too much time on the 'managing' function.
   c   Using Figure 1 as a yardstick, I spend too much time on the 'operating' function.
   d   Where my job is concerned, I regard the percentages in Figure 1 as unrealistic.   (   )

5 Again, being an honest injun, do you find yourself getting bogged-down with routine tasks?
   a   Yes, all too often.
   b   Yes, fairly often.
   c   Once in a blue moon.
   d   No, never.   (   )

6 By all that you hold sacred, how prone are you to the *mañana* syndrome – putting things off until tomorrow?
   a   Never, ever.
   b   Occasionally.
   c   I'm very prone to this.   (   )

7 Considering such factors as economic crises, changing attitudes, narrowing pay differentials, the general devaluation of your other perks, etc., how do you rate your personal prestige at work?
   a   It's virtually non-existent.
   b   It's subject to continual erosion.
   c   As 'average' and unchanging.
   d   I've no worries on this score – it's consistently high.
   e   I never think about it – and hence am not concerned about its 'quality'.
   f   It's poor – an important factor being the quality of my perform-ance.   (   )

8 Do you tend to worry about your job security?
   a   No, never.
   b   In today's climate, I'd be a fool not to worry about it – and I do.
   c   Yes, I worry a great deal – mainly because, if I'm truthful, I can't trust my employer to be 'dead straight' where my job is concerned.

> *d*   Yes, I worry a great deal about my job – because, in my heart of hearts, I know I'm not really good at it.   (   )

9   Regarding your subordinates –
> *a*   They are all extremely proficient, and I have every confidence in their ability to cope with anything I put their way.
> *b*   Being human, they're of average skill and proficiency, which means that there's the odd 'very good' and 'not so good' feature of their overall performance. I've no real problems.
> *c*   Despite all my efforts at encouraging, training and disciplining, I'm saddled with subordinates who simply will not make any effort to improve – otherwise, things are okay.
> *d*   I have the misfortune to be cursed with the worst bunch of subordinates in creation.   (   )

10   Regarding your job –
> *a*   It is my life – it totally absorbs me, and I dislike being away from it.
> *b*   I like it and I'm good at it – but there are other things in life.
> *c*   I'm an average person doing an averagely good job of work.
> *d*   I do my best, but I don't particularly enjoy my job.
> *e*   I hate the bloody thing.   (   )

Before we look at your responses, I had better state the obvious; namely, that the questionnaire is not intended to provide you with an instant rating of your personal immunity to under-delegation – we'll leave that kind of rubbish well alone. Quite simply, my aim is to provoke you into using your selected 'answers' as *triggers for thought* – so let us do exactly that. Pick out whichever comments are appropriate from the following list, and think in as near-objective terms as possible about each one, remembering that your honour-bound task is to discover the truth.

Question 1

a   Your 'very confident' decision that you are not guilty of under-delegation tells me that you should have had little difficulty in coming up with rosy-type responses throughout the question-naire. We shall see. . . . For the moment, suffice it to say without appearing *too* sceptical that Sod's Law has a special provision relating to over-confidence. They call it come-uppance.

b   Your choice of 'fairly confident' indicates some doubt – and, if only as a prophylactic measure, dictates that you conduct a pretty searching appraisal of your performance in delegating work to others. However, the mere fact that you are reading this book could mean that you are already aware of this need. . . .

c or *d*   Full marks for your element of frankness in electing for either of these alternatives. Be assured, there are some practical tips coming up later – and, of course, it could well be the case that this questionnaire will help to pinpoint the source(s) of your difficulty.

Question 2

a   Does that make two *a*'s thus far? With such confidence, it should do, even if the 'six months' bit is not quite accurate. Let's see how things progress from here on. . . .

b or *c*   For the purposes of this exercise, I'm afraid there is very little difference between these two responses. In fact, in cases where the cap fits (not you, reader – perish the thought), either alternative can serve as a 'conscience-easer', can't it? Think about it.

d   Another honest response – which, of course, must pose a very relevant question. *Why* have you never discussed 'delegation loads' with your subordinates? Is it really the case that the idea just didn't occur to you, or is there a more significant reason?

Question 3

a   If, indeed, you are not required to formally appraise your subordinates, then, fair enough – you are off this particular hook.

b   Firstly, if you did come up with *a*-type selections for Questions 1 and 2 – well, on the surface, all is fine. Even at this early stage, a picture is beginning to emerge which does you very much credit . . . .

Secondly, if your responses do not reflect this acme of perfection, then now is the time to start thinking in very serious terms about under-delegation. It is my hope that your organization is sufficiently enlightened to require *open* appraisal of subordinates – and, if this is the case, the all-important appraisal discussions should have been used as a vehicle for, among other things, a detailed and frank look at delegation with the individuals concerned. So, if your scheme is an open system, here was the opportunity and the *requirement* for the discussions which, according to your response in Question 2, are either a hazy (and improbable?) memory, or didn't occur at all. As an afterthought, even your report writing within a *closed* appraisal system should have prompted you to take some action where under-delegation is concerned. . . . Think on't.

Question 4

a   Once again, near-perfection personified. What more can one say, except congratulations?

b   Overmuch time spent on the 'managing' function may, if anything, point to the fact that you *over*-delegate – and we will be dealing with that equally pernicious aspect in the next chapter.

c   We are now approaching the crunch – and I'm sure you will not need reminding that excessive time spent by a manager on the 'operating' function is a prime cause of under-delegation.

d   Bearing in mind that the percentages in Figure 1 can only represent an approximate yardstick, I am not going to quibble over moderate differences of opinion. However, if you reject them as totally unrealistic, then stand by for a mighty rap on the knuckles – because, if there is anyone out of step, *it is you*. All the basic principles and 'rules' of management are subject to a wide variety of interpretations and applications in practice, but this does not include outright rejection by any maverick-manager who happens along. Point taken?

Question 5

a   I hope that you selected alternative *c* in Question 4 – and, on reflection, I'm sure you did. . . . Enough said.

b   If you do get bogged down fairly often with routine tasks, then, once again, we have a significant pointer to the fact that you under-delegate. As a preliminary to tackling the drill which comes later, give some thought to the question of what type of routine work creates the hiccup – and ask yourself who among your subordinates is best qualified to take it over. If there is no one so suited, why not?

c   And who doesn't get bogged down once in a blue moon with routine tasks? If this selected response represents the true state of affairs, then hey-ho for sweet normality!

d   Hum, tell you what –I don't believe you.

Question 6

a   Y'know, at the risk of being quite rude, this really is getting a bit too good to be true. However, I must confess that I once met a manager-character who was absolutely free of all such human failings as occasionally putting things off until tomorrow. Unfortunately, this paragon of virtue happened also to be a dead-fish, automaton of a man whom everyone healthily despised . . . .

b   Again, a human par for the course, and signifying nothing sinister – provided it remains an occasional resort to *mañana*.

c   An excessive use of the pending tray is often a concomitant cause of under-delegation – and, for the umpteenth time, it would be wise for you to engage in some serious heart-searching. Depend on it, other people do notice the *mañana* syndrome, and it is usually only a matter of time before someone in authority reacts in a violent and unpleasant fashion.

Question 7

a or *b*   Having elected for either of these alternatives, you are plainly concerned about the level of your prestige at work – and it could be that this concern is causing you, albeit unconsciously, to 'reinforce' your position by keeping work to yourself, instead of more properly delegating it to others. The odds are this is what is happening.

c   No worries here – except, perhaps, to express an element of curiosity over your apparent content with an 'average' assessment at, er, anything?

d   I am reminded that one gentleman who rated his personal prestige as consistently high and, as a consequence, didn't worry at all about it, was Benito Mussolini. It is worth recalling what happened to him.

e   This, if I may make so bold, could qualify as your biggest fib of the year. Think about it.

f   This is an utterly frank response, and it is my hope that your candour is matched by a similar level of determination to do something about retrieving the situation. Let's face it, achieving a personal *awareness* of poor performance is tantamount to taking the first step on the road to improving it. *It can be done* – so, do not falter, and make delegation one of your prime considerations.

Question 8

a   If, as you have confirmed, you *never* worry about your job security, you are a rare person, indeed. It is to be hoped that, in addition to enjoying such equanimity, you are also blessed with perfect hearing and reflexes – for that faint rustle in the air could be a quick bullet, winging its way you-know-where.

b, *c* or *d*   Again, for the purposes of this questionnaire, there is precious little difference between these three alternatives. It is a fact that worry over one's job security, be it based on fact or fancy, can trigger many managers into that Catch-22 situation of striving to be indispensable, with the consequence that under-delegation becomes the automatic order of the day.

Question 9

a or *b*   The difference between these two alternatives is purely one of degree; while we would all like a supremely proficient bunch of subordinates, most of us get what the distribution curve dictates – average people doing an averagely good job. If, however, your staff are the acme of perfection, are you quite certain that your delegation matches up to their very high level of proficiency and expectations?

As for the average staff with their human share of ups and downs performance-wise, do you perhaps under-delegate in terms of providing insufficient challenge for the skills at which they are good – and inadequate training by experience to cater for and improve their lesser abilities?

c or *d* So far as these responses are concerned, there is no good to be served by my offering sympathy with your lot, or any other form of palliative. I call to mind the words of an old management buff: 'There are no bad injuns, only bad chiefs' – and commend them to your attention. This bald homily spells nothing but truth for the manager who, having failed after every effort to bring subordinates up to scratch, then chickens out of getting rid of his encumbrances. The executive who is willing to put up with such a situation is the classic under-delegator, and he or she deserves putting down. Incidentally, one familiar bleat by such mismanagers in the UK is: 'Huh, you don't know what you're talking about! With all this unfair dismissal business hanging over my head, I daren't sack anyone.' To which unreasoned outburst there is but one reply – rubbish! Despite emotive charges by some management die-hards about draconian law, biassed tribunals and what-not, an employer retains the right to sack any employee – all the law requires is that a dismissal shall be warranted and actioned throughout in accordance with simple requirements. And *natural justice* is one of 'em. . . .

Question 10

a If you opted for this response, you will probably know what I am going to say – are you so all-fired interested in your job that you've commited the cardinal sin of selfishly appropriating that which is rightly your subordinates' work? If you don't know the answer to this one, be brave enough to discuss it *with them* – and be prepared for a jolting surprise.

b, c or *d* Whichever of this particular trio you have selected, it all boils down to one thing – have you jerked yourself into a consistently right frame of mind over delegation, or is there a chance that a certain lack of interest or motivation on your part is, in fact, causing you to under-delegate?

e By opting for this response, you force me to put aside my reference to delegation in favour of one, sixty-thousand-dollar question – if you hate your job, why in tarnation are you still in the chair? I suppose your likely answer is that you can't afford to give it up – and, if that is the case, my reaction must be that you are a brass-bound, disgusting villain. However much you may aver that you do not allow your intense dislike for your work to affect your management of others, I say – nuts. I pity your subordinates, and hope that *your* boss will soon lose those blinkers and load his gun. . . .

Please do remember, I said 'triggers for thought' – and if that little lot has failed to get you thinking about yourself in relation to the vexed business of under-delegation, then I rate it as a fair bet that nothing will. It is now time to move on to the second and, dare I say it, pretty demanding self-tutorial – demanding, that is, if you really wish to check your delegation state of health, and do something about eradicating any consequent nasties.

Self-tutorial

Step-by-step measures to remedy under-delegation

For my money, the best way to tackle the detection and cure of any tendency to under-delegate is to resort to that well-known management method known as the six-step problem-solving process – a somewhat high-hat name for a very simple and effective approach to any executive brain-teaser.

- *Step 1 – Identify the problem*

All right, we know it well, but it is worth repeating – the probability, if not dead certainty, that 'Manager X' (this being a tactful move to spare your further blushes) under-delegates work.

- *Step 2 – Gather all the relevant facts*

There is little doubt that this could prove to be a time-consuming and tedious task; but if the end-result is to be of any use at all, we must take every care to draw together all the factors which have a bearing on Manager X's predicament – for predicament it is. It is for this reason that I have devoted all the preceding text in this chapter to identifying and highlighting the five main causes of under-delegation. What we now have to do is decide which one (or more) is relevant to our anonymous executive – who, one dares to hope, has also seen fit to answer the questionnaire. . . .

Firstly and obviously, it is necessary for Manager X to copy your example and engage in a period of frank introspection. On the basis of the gut-feelings engendered by his responses, he will have a pretty good idea of his personal hang-ups:

Lethargy	– Relevant?
Concern for prestige	– Relevant?
Fear of being superseded	– Relevant?
Lack of confidence in subordinates	– Relevant?
A consuming interest in the job	– Relevant?

Then, having used this spell of candid thought to isolate certain or probable causes of his malady, Manager X should plunge into a second mental exercise – this time endeavouring to think in detailed, objective terms about each subordinate in turn:

What are his/her strengths and weaknesses?

To what extent have I exploited strengths – and, just as vital, taken action to overcome weaknesses?

In what areas have I signally failed to take full advantage of his/her strengths?

Does it appear necessary that I will have to modify his/her other tasks in order to derive this fuller advantage?

The final phase in gathering all the relevant facts is one which Manager X, being a very human animal, may well decide to ignore – the business of actually conferring with the subordinates concerned. A probable excuse for avoiding this salient responsibility will be something along the lines that such action will tend to weaken friend X's management position in the eyes of his staff – to which the answer is, baloney. A properly conducted discussion (of which more anon) on what the subordinate *is* doing in terms of delegated tasks, and what he/she *could* do if given the chance, will do much to establish the true facts of the situation.

- **Step 3 – Establish the cause of the problem**

By this time the specific cause(s) of Manager X's problem ought to be self-evident, but it is by no means certain that this will be the case. One hard fact of problem-solving life is that technical failures are capable of far easier and quicker solutions than are human puzzles, which can be much more complex. Relatively few of us are inclined to admit, even in the sanctuary of our own thoughts, that there is something seriously awry with this or that much-nurtured, personal outlook or habit – and, of course, when it comes to establishing prowess at delegation, that's exactly what Manager X (or anyone else, if you see what I mean) is required to do.

- **Step 4 – Search for and develop all the possible solutions**

It really isn't our hero's day – for, in seeking out and developing all the possible solutions, the first thing he will discover is a dismal shortage of convenient, half-measure bolt-holes in which to hide. By way of illustration, let us list some of these stern, all-or-nothing remedies:

LETHARGY

There is only one answer to this one, but how do we get over to Manager X that all he has to do is virtually change his personality and become a paragon of virtue – or, more to the point and short of standing over him with an outsize whip, how do we actually make him undergo this magic change for the better?

The obvious fact is, we can't. Apart from impressing the vital need for our lethargic leopard to acquire new spots, all that can be done is to offer some guidelines for success – along with an earnest prayer that the message will have its desired effect. Sad to say, human nature being what it is, it probably won't – but, for all that, we have to make an effort:

'Manager X, if you don't buck your ideas up, then, as sure as God made little apples, sooner or later you'll get the sack. And everyone will rejoice to see you go. . . .'

'Here, in a nutshell, is what you must do:
    Examine each and every aspect of your work.
    Divide it into segments, and evaluate each one in terms of success or failure.
    Set realistic objectives in each case.
    Categorize all your tasks in terms of 'managing' and 'operating' functions.
    Assess the actual capabilities of each subordinate.
    Decide which 'operating' tasks can be delegated, and to whom.
    And, having ploughed through this book, delegate fairly and squarely.
    Work at all times like the new person you have become.'

'Our prayers are private, but they are for your success.'

CONCERN FOR PRESTIGE

Manager X has just got to accept that, while the maintenance of personal prestige may be important, it must not be garnered at the expense of selfishly hanging on to every jot and tittle of work that crops up. Oddly enough, the manager who is thus afflicted with an overweening concern for prestige appears to completely overlook the fact that, by consistently under-delegating, his reputation will rapidly come to stink in his subordinates' nostrils – and, boy, will they publish their views abroad. . . . Perhaps it is this fact which will serve to convince the Manager X's of the world that they are playing with a truly Catch-22 situation.

Anyway, this thing called prestige is much like a balloon – too much puffing at it, and it'll go bang.

FEAR OF BEING SUPERSEDED

The fear of losing one's job comes in two forms: firstly, that which is founded in fact (warnings of poor performance, and so on); and secondly, that which is the product of imagined or 'estimated' insecurity. ('He's redundant today and, by the way things are going, it'll be my turn tomorrow.') In the former case, Manager X is clearly on probation and the solution is usually in his own hands. So far as the latter, imagined, fear is concerned – well, I'm no trick-cyclist, are you? But hold on a tick, there is one thing we can assert with absolute accuracy and all the authority we can command:

'Manager X, regardless of whether your fear is real or imagined, it is little short of criminal to try to make yourself indispensable by under-delegating work. So do take your sticky fingers out of your subordinates' rightful pies.'

LACK OF CONFIDENCE IN ONE'S SUBORDINATES

Once again, it is very difficult for us to develop this particular solution to any great effect – for, at the risk of boring repetition, the remedy rests firmly in Manager X's hands. We can, however, fire a barrage of mindful home-truths:

'More often than not, lack of trust in one's subordinates is founded in unhealthy fancy, and it is to be hoped that, deep down, the scallywag so afflicted will recognize the ailment – and do something about it, like delegating work.'

'Harking back to the body of this chapter, if Manager X's lack of trust is founded in fact – then, whatever the cause, IT IS HIS FAULT. He should start acting like a manager and put things right in his ailing bailiwick – so that, again fulfilling his role as manager, he can delegate fairly and well.'

● *Step 5 – Implement the most practical solution*

One hears a great deal from the pundits* about the constant need for executives who control people to subject themselves to what is popularly known as 'attitude-changing'. This most innocuous of terms, pronounced trippingly on the tongue, tends to belie the dire magnitude of its import; namely, the requirement for the poor old manager to grab that thing we call personality, give it a furious pounding – and emerge, like a butterfly from the chrysalis, a completely new creature. In this context, the cold, hard light of experience provides us with some pointers:

'Woe and more woe – for once, the pundits are right.'

'Most of us do need to change our attitudes.'

'But doing so is just about as difficult as sprouting wings.'

It will not have escaped your notice that the remedies for the various ills of under-delegation all involve . . . yes, that's right, attitude-changing. The way managers regard their cloistered world of work, the manner in which they ply their deeply held prejudices, beliefs and expectations, will depend absolutely on the sum and substance of their individual personalities – but, sadly and as we all know, the constituent characteristics are stamped by Nature with well-nigh indelible ink. Few of us enjoy being poked in the personality midriff and told that we are lacking in this or that quality – for, way down under, no one knows us as well as we know ourselves, and heaven help the impudent blighter who dares to suggest otherwise.

---

* *Pundit*: a learned Hindu. In management, some would say: a person who, finding it difficult to practise the art, elects to teach it; one who uses stationery with a 'Management Consultant' letterhead; a calculating author with an eye to a good thing. . . .

Well, hard luck. Such finer feelings may nourish the temperament, but they can do nothing but drastically inhibit, if not destroy, a manager's chances of genuine success. Returning to our theme, any ploy directed at eradicating the under-delegation bug must, perforce, involve a hefty and effective bout of attitude-changing. It's as simple *and* difficult as that.

- *Step 6 – Evaluate the results*

Of all the steps in the problem-solving process, this is the one that most managers neglect. Certainly, in the context of sorting out delegation weaknesses, it is absolutely vital to keep a continuing eye on results – otherwise the rot will set in with a vengeance and, fine resolutions or not, the executive concerned will find himself in a worse position than when he first set foot on the self-improvement trail. It is bad enough being known and acknowledged by one's subordinates as a poor delegator; but when a detailed attempt to put things right is limelighted by public failure – then, that is a disaster of no mean proportions.

And now, something on that 'delegation discussion'

For the purposes of this exercise, imagine that Willy (your typical manager, if there is such a beast) is pretty certain that he is guilty of under-delegating work to Joe, his supervisor – and, ergo, there comes the moment when he decides to put this part of his executive house in order. To this laudable end, let us further imagine that Willy holds a discussion on the subject with his Man Friday, and that you are privy to snippets of what he says.

Your task, for which you will again require pencil and paper, *is to consider in the light of the circumstances the relative merit or otherwise of what you overhear.* Makes notes on the various comments-cum-questions and, when you have gone through them all, compare your observations with the answer-clues that follow. So here goes . . .

1 'Joe, I've asked you in for a chat because I'm pretty certain that I don't delegate enough work your way. . . .'

2 'Come in, Joe – and take a seat. Look, I'd like your views on something that's been bothering me of late. . . . What d'you think of the amount of work I push in your direction?'

3 'Joe, I'll come straight to the point. You're my Number Two in the department – and, quite honestly, I think you should undertake more of my day-to-day, routine work than is presently the case. . . .'

4 'In my book, Joe, a supervisor should discharge responsibilities and exercise authority at least commensurate with his position. . . . Now, you're my supervisor – so, in this regard, how d'you think you're coping at present?'

5 'Tell me, Joe – what are your feelings about your present levels of responsibility and authority?'

6 'Joe, I've been thinking quite a bit of late about the way in which I tackle my job – and, to be honest, I've come to the conclusion that I'm guilty of under-delegation where you're concerned. I'd like to hear what you have to say. . . .'

7 'Joe, do I delegate enough work to you?'

8 'Joe, what are your views on under-delegation?'

9 'I don't mind telling you, Joe, what with all those redundancies last year and the way things are going in general, I've been a pretty worried man security-wise – and, as a result, I reckon it's true to say that I've tended to hog certain aspects of my job, and at your expense. What I'm trying to say is. . . .'

10 'There's something I've been meaning to get round to for months, and that's the re-organization of your responsibilities and duties. Now, what I intend to do is . . .'

All right, let us now see how your notes compare with the following answer-clues – remembering, of course, that we are dealing with a pretty subjective exercise, and opinions will vary like the March winds. What we are after are *pointers* in the right direction, nothing more.

1 While fairly well on track, the wording of this opener (*'I'm pretty certain that I don't delegate enough work your way.'*) could well trigger Joe into thinking he is being accused of idleness – which, however true, is not the object of Willy's exercise. This very common habit of 'shifting the onus', be it wilful or completely unintentional, is totally reprehensible and should be avoided like the plague.

2 Yes, of course, open-ended questions are the thing, but this one is far too open-ended. The question, *'What d'you think of the amount of work I push in your direction?'* is capable of more than one interpretation, and such ambiguity is bad. For instance, once again, Joe could not be blamed for regarding the query as a possible lead-in to criticism of his performance – in which event, he might well 'go on the defensive' from the outset.

3 Here, in Joe's eyes, we have another possible implication that he is not fully pulling his weight. Albeit unintentional, Willy's businesslike and somewhat brusque approach smacks of the accusatory, rather than the discursive. If, as is almost certainly the case in real-life situations, Joe is painfully aware of Willy's shortcomings as a delegator, he will not admire his boss's slightly snide mode of approach.

4 Willy has started with a pretty fair opening comment, for all that it is

wordy and pompous, but he then goes on to ruin his good intention. . . . The question, *'Now you're my supervisor – so, in this regard, how d'you think you're coping at present?'* has, once again, 'shifted the onus' and cannot fail to put Joe on his guard.

5 *If* Willy, despite his weakness in delegation, enjoys some respect where Joe is concerned, and *if* he voices this question with sincerity and with the right look on his face – then, for my money, Joe may well come up with some useful views. If, however, our Willy is an unrespected clot of a manager – well, he'll probably deserve what he gets. . . .

6 Again, this approach will depend for its merit on whether or not Joe respects his boss as a man, let alone as a manager. If he does, then Willy's admission of his failing will probably prompt Joe's admiration – and, so far as he is able to give it, his willing help and support. If, on the other hand, Joe has little respect for his senior, then it is likely that the whole session will go for a ball of chalk.

7 A direct question – destined to prompt a 'yes', 'no', or equally unproductive answer. Remember the 'magic-six formula' for ensuring that all questions are open-ended and, hence, worth the asking:
   What . . .   Why . . .   When . . .
   Which . . .   Where . . .   How . . .

8 The value of the question, *'Joe, what are your views on under-delegation?'* will plainly depend on the context in which it is posed. Used as a trigger for discussion, it could be said to have merit – but, on the occasion in question, when it is fair to assume that Willy has already pinpointed his personal weakness, it is his views that really count, not those of his supervisor. However, once the purpose of the session has been resolved, and if time permits, there is no harm and some potential benefit to be sought by thus widening the discussion. After all, Joe's personal career development, if nothing else, requires that he should consider and understand the practice and associated complications of management techniques.

9 Frankness is one thing, spreading alarm and despondency is quite another. . . . It stands out a mile (at least, I hope it does) that Willy is quite wrong to address Joe in such defeatist and demotivating terms. One of the most important responsibilities of 'high office', and I use that term very loosely, is never, ever to share one's doubts and fears about work with one's subordinates – it can do much harm and absolutely no good. For all that most managers are well aware of this fact, many still succumb to the temptation of thus leaning on their subordinates' shoulders. . . .

10 Pride comes before a fall – and the miscreant manager who is intent on wrapping his own shortcomings within a highly dodgy veneer of 'I'm

going to re-organize *your* lot in life' deserves all he gets. We'll pretend Willy never came out with this one. I mean, you would never attempt such a ploy, would you?

One aim in this exercise in 'delegation discussion' is to remind you, as if you needed reminding, that the question of a manager's personality obviously rears its head in all such real-life, discursive activities – as, indeed, it does in everything he does. *Attitude-changing,* eh?

3 Even bigger warts

> It was truly a splendid structure, and Yossarian throbbed with a
> mighty sense of accomplishment each time he gazed at it and
> reflected that none of the work that had gone into it was his.
>
> Joseph Heller
> *Catch-22*

For my sins, over the past few years I have had the good and, on the odd
occasion, rankly bad fortune to represent employers and ex-employees in a
fairly mixed bag of industrial tribunal cases. Although this activity has
provided me with some valuable experience, to say nothing of scars, the
conclusion of each case has never failed to leave me feeling utterly dispirited
– for, win or lose, the tribunal arena is probably the saddest and, at times,
certainly the most sickening aspect of the British employment scene. Now,
lest you wonder what on earth such an observation has to do with
delegation, let me hasten to explain.

It was while casting round in my mind for ways and means of introducing
this chapter that I suddenly recalled, in typical grasshopper fashion and for
no reason at all, one such sad tribunal involvement – and, in the same moment
realized that I had found my desired 'opener'. Suffice it to say that the hearing
involved a complaint of unfair dismissal, and that much of the applicant's
submission was concerned with a single piece of paper; namely, his ex-
employer's formal statement of the reasons why he had been dismissed.
Here, cloaked in suitable anonymity, is the document in question:

THE ABACUS ENGINEERING COMPANY LTD
IRON HOUSE CASTLE HILL CAMBRIDGE CB1 2AP

5 January 1984   Tel: Cambridge 764532

G.L.Blanchard Esq
14 Orchard Way
Huntingdon, Cambs

Dear Mr Blanchard

STATEMENT OF REASONS FOR YOUR DISMISSAL

We acknowledge receipt of your letter dated 1 January 1984. The reasons for
your dismissal on 31 December 1983 from the post of Sales Manager with
this Company are as follows:

Lack of capability for performing work of the kind which you were employed to do, in that, despite two formal warnings given to you on 22 August 1983 and 31 October 1983, you persisted in allocating an undue number of managerial tasks which were rightly and wholly your personal responsibility to subordinate members of staff; thereby involving the employees concerned in work for which, by virtue of their appointments and levels of authority, they were grossly unqualified.

During an interview conducted by the Sales Director, Mr W. Hill, on 23 December 1983, you agreed that, despite the two previous warnings and contrary to the undertaking provided by you on each of these occasions to rectify matters, you had so neglected your responsibilities as an executive of this Company. You further agreed that there were no mitigating circumstances to be taken into account. You were then informed by Mr Hill that the Company had no alternative but to dismiss you from your appointment as Sales Manager, a decision which was upheld by the Managing Director, Mr H. Swales, following your subsequent appeal.

I enclose a letter from the Trustees of the Pension Fund, and would ask you to kindly give this your early attention.

Yours sincerely

J. Hawkes
Personnel Manager

This errant manager deserved to bite the dust, and bite the dust he did. I should add that the chairman of the industrial tribunal concerned made no bones in his summing-up about the wanton manner in which the applicant had over-delegated his duties. Needless to say, the complaint of unfair dismissal failed – and no one (including, I suspect, the applicant) was unduly surprised by this unanimous decision.

Over-delegation, is the other and almost-certainly worst end of the delegation weakness spectrum. .... I say 'worst' because, although under-delegation leaves staff metaphorically twiddling their thumbs, there is a chance that those with any motivation at all will compensate for the failings of their seniors by seeking out time-filling and productive work. However, for the staff who suffer the slings and arrows of over-delegation, there is usually no alternative – for relatively few such unfortunates will attempt to seek official redress or, bigger step still, cry 'enough is enough' and leave their overworked jobs.

Before taking a detailed look at the various causes and effects of over-delegation, a word on tactics. Having stressed and stressed again in the previous chapter the need for your candid introspection when ploughing through the various bits and pieces, suffice it to say that an exactly similar approach is required in relation to this section of our study. You and I both know just how easy it is to adopt an impersonal stance when reading about human attitudes and weaknesses. The oft-automatic reaction, 'Ah, yes, too right – but it doesn't apply to me,' can be an extremely handy let-out, pandering to the self-same vanity that prompts a goodly chunk of the trouble in the first place. So, once again, do think in essentially personal terms. . . .

Inadequate knowledge/experience

If every manager had Dr Laurence J. Peter's flash of intuitive reasoning engraved on his or her heart, the world of work would not only be a much safer environment in which to earn one's daily bread – it would be a stack more efficient, to boot. Allow me to remind you of the sterling and total truth of the Peter Principle:*

In a hierarchy every employee tends to rise to his level of incompetence.

It is an inescapable fact that the vast majority of people are promoted to better positions almost exclusively on the basis of past performance, with little or no attention paid by the promoters to an objective assessment of their likely future competence. Putting it bluntly, far too many managers who are good at certain jobs get hoicked out of them and placed in more senior posts – where, given a month of Sundays, they just cannot hope to cope. Consider your own organization, reader, and I guarantee you will not have to look very far before stumbling over undeniable products of the Peter Principle – and, be it noted, that is before you even start to engage in that candid self-appraisal, isn't it?

The manager who is equipped with insufficient knowledge or experience to cope effectively with a job has, nevertheless, to survive in the work-jungle. One very tempting 'solution' is to hive off (either with premeditation, or in the virtual form of a reflex, defensive action) the nasty tasks to others – and, more often than not, this entails clobbering subordinates with an undeserved and ill-administered dose of over-delegation.

In passing, it is wise to remember that the term 'inadequate knowledge/ experience' can cover a number of specific areas of weakness:

- Lack of *technical* knowledge/experience – the detailed know-how of the job concerned.

- Lack of *general management* knowledge/experience – the 'across-the-board' know-how of managing the Three Ms (Men, Money and Materials).

---

* *The Peter Principle: Why Things Go Wrong*, by Dr Laurence J. Peter and Raymond Hull (William Morrow & Co., New York, 1969), could be said to constitute the Book of Revelations in the Management Bible.

- Defects of *personality* – for example, the person who achieves what others construe as an effective rapport with his subordinates when working at supervisor level, may well turn out to be wholly unable to fulfil the communications role when sitting in a more senior post.

Laziness

In the preceding chapter we noted how one brand of laziness can be the root cause of rabid under-delegation, but here is another form – the well-nigh despicable indolence that triggers a manager to evade this and that responsibility by merely transferring the tasks concerned onto the shoulders of hapless subordinates. Many moons ago an old management buff told me that roughly one in three executives over-delegate for reasons of personal laziness – and, having mingled with quite a few managers over the ensuing years, I think he was just about right. The same old sage also reminded me of the corollary to his statement; namely, that anyone who has worked for three different bosses has suffered at least once from the effects of such over-delegation – and, on looking back at the way things went for me, he was right on that one, too.

The only realistic hope is that, sooner or later (preferably sooner), the Nemesis of the quick bullet will thud into the quivering flesh of every lazy manager-tyke that you and I know, and so despise.

Lack of motivation

While it is all very fine for authorities on management to stress that we should always be the shining light of example in all things to our subordinates, such a heady pronouncement takes little account of the fact that managers, like other people, are only human after all. I would therefore offer that there is at least some excuse for the unhappy employee who, plonked into an executive seat by a coercive and uncaring boss, is so demotivated that his or her interest in the job is just about nil – and, as a result, undue portions of work end up being delegated to subordinates. Witness . . .

'When he first mentioned the prospect of my promotion to an office-based job, I told him straight away that I wasn't really interested. The fact is, I've spent most of my working life out on some sales-patch or other, because selling's what I like doing – and it's what I'm good at. . . . But, no, in his eyes, that counted for nothing – all he wanted was to get me in that flamin' office. . . . Of course, I saw the red light in the end – it was either go along with his wishes, or get out. . . . So, here I am – stuck in a job that I don't really enjoy, with absolutely nothing in the way of help

APROPOS OF SOMETHING No. 3

'Ah, Ron, just the person. . . . Look, there's that wretched meeting of the Amenities Committee this afternoon. . . . I'm going to be tied up all day – I wonder if you'd be a good chap and stand in for me? There're no problems – it's just that someone from the department ought to put in an appearance, if y'know what I mean. . . .'

More often than not, such delegated 'instructions' (for, as we all know, those charming words, 'I wonder if you'd be a good chap and do this or that,' do constitute an instruction) to act as an unrehearsed stand-in are the prelude to yet another demonstration of management inefficiency. The poor Joe concerned – or, in this example, Ron – shoves existing work aside and duly attends the meeting, destined to lend about as much participation as that to be expected from an Egyptian mummy. If and when the victim of this crass act of delegation does happen to open his mouth, it'll probably sound something like:

'Er, well – I'm afraid I don't know the answer to that one. . . .' or *'Only Mr Codpiece can help you out on that – but I'm afraid he couldn't make it this afternoon. He sent me, instead. . . .'*

To quote the poet – d'you know what I mean?

or support from him or the MD. To tell you the honest truth, I've had it up to here
. . . .

(A sad admission by a 'manager' who, when pressed, readily admitted that he was prone to over-delegating work.)

Observe, if you will, that I am only suggesting there can be mitigating circumstances where demotivated over-delegators are concerned. The offence of thus loading one's subordinates remains reprehensible, whatever the basic cause, and a plea of demotivation cannot let a manager off the hook. As is so often the case, the cure for such trouble is firmly in the hands of those further up the line – whose responsibility it is to ensure that every employee, and most certainly every manager, is possessed of the requisite fire in the belly.

Demotivation is one thing, but when there is nothing there in the first place – well, that's quite another ball-game. A further provision of Sod's inimitable law dictates that, every so often, there is promoted to the seat of management a character who, by virtue of his or her utter, ingrained laziness, makes a profession of feeding on the efforts of others. You may feel inclined to agree with my continued amazement that so many of these wretched leeches manage, by hook or by crook, to hold down their respective jobs – which, of course, is a direct indictment of the bosses concerned. I say, to the wall with them.

Last but not least, there is the brand of laziness to which you and I *are* sadly prone – best described as the mini-devil who, sitting on our shoulders, tempts us every now and again to hive off this or that unpleasant, unenjoyed task onto poor Joe Subordinate. Be honest, we all do it, and we damned well shouldn't.

Aspects of fear

It may be difficult for the executive who enjoys a healthy, all-round self-confidence to understand that there are managers who, quite literally, suffer continued, ever-gnawing fear at work. Fear of the boss, fear of some (or all) colleagues and/or subordinates, fear of getting the sack, fear of the job itself – all of these several anxieties, be they triggered by real or imagined situations, can lead to skimping of a manager's personal responsibilities by simple resort to over-delegation. When, as at the time of writing this book, good jobs are at a premium, the timorous executive (to say nothing of the normally resilient character) may go through a virtual hell of fear at work – and, given this, subordinates can and do suffer.

Enough is known of the domineering, fear-inducing type of boss, fear of the job, and the sack – but spare a thought for this business of fear of one's peers and/or juniors. It was the Danish zoologist Thorleif Schjelderup-Ebbe (yes, that's right, Schjelderup-Ebbe . . .) who first coined the principle of the Pecking Order, and, as we are well aware, the human animal is just as prone to the thing as his companion species. The organization hierarchy, with its well-defined levels of authority, may become much less relevant when a timid manager is faced with a peer or subordinate who imposes the stamp of a dominant personality on their working relationship. It often happens that such a persuasive colleague – or, even worse, a dominant junior who literally takes control – will blow the whistle for over-delegation to occur.

Whether generated by fear or its near-equivalent, over-anxiety to please, the resultant overloading of subordinates is, again, nothing short of reprehensible.

A postscript

If, as I am confident is the case, you ploughed dutifully through the questionnaire in the preceding chapter, it should be clear that most of the items are equally relevant in establishing whether or not you, reader, are guilty of practising over-delegation. However, before plunging back to the questionnaire (because that, quite simply, is what you should be thinking of doing), it might be a good idea to focus your mind again on the four main over-delegation bugs:

Inadequate knowledge/experience
Laziness
Lack of motivation
Aspects of fear

Now, dragging your conscience by the ears into the open light of home-truth, do you not already have a pretty good idea of the state of your health? It is possible that a few prompts are in order . . .

1 Exactly what is your breadth of technical knowledge where your job is concerned?

2 To what extent do you regularly read-up on new developments and technological change?

3 When did you last attend a course or presentation on 'something new', or even a revisional session on an existing process or system?

4 How often do you get the nasty, sinking feeling that your experience is leaving you ill-equipped to deal with this or that situation?

5 And, if you are thus affected, what are you doing about it?

6 You will know in that heart of hearts if you are infected with laziness – but, apart from reading this book, what are you doing to put things right?

7 And is it going to be like all those other, laughable New Year resolutions – and fade away into nothing?

8 If you feel lacking in motivation, however caused, when are you going to stop crying in your beer? Have you forgotten exactly how short life is – and do you intend to continue thus to prostitute your morale?

9 If you experience fear at work, to what extent is the degree of your anxiety justified by the facts of the situation? Consider Rudyard Kipling's glorious discovery, *'What matter? I have killed Fear'* – and set out to do exactly that. Given the resolution, it can be done.

10 So, we come to the crunch question. Have these prompts embarrassed you into realizing, *as realize you must*, that the four main over-delegation bugs are very cogent and real dangers – not only to your poor subordinates, but to your own, precious working existence?

Grab another coffee – it's hey-ho for the self-tutorial.

Self-tutorial

Exercise nit-pick

By now, the mere glimpse of the word 'self-tutorial' should have you reaching for paper and pencil – so, while pretending that you are thus all set to go, do creep stealthily to the sideboard and dig them out, will you? The purpose of this little exercise is to set you thinking about this and that – all you have to do is consider the following statements (some of which you will have heard many times before) and note down your reaction to each one in terms of its general validity. We'll compare notes at the end of the tutorial.

1 'I never expect my people to do anything I can't do myself.'

2 'While delegation may be a spur to employee commitment, it has the disadvantage of making junior members of staff feel more important.'

3 'In delegation, it is logical that it sometimes takes longer for a manager to tell someone what to do than it takes to complete the job personally.'

4 'As a manager, one of the advantages of delegation is that you are preparing yourself for promotion.'

5 'In delegation, authority and accountability are inseparable.'

6 'When I delegate work, I ensure that the people concerned know that they are totally responsible for the outcome.'

7 'Delegation is simply the act of passing on to a subordinate some aspect of the work that a manager is himself expected to carry out.'

8 'There's no such thing as over-delegation – staff need to be stretched to the utmost of their capabilities.'

Remember, hang on to your notes – you'll need them soon enough.

A touch of organization

One of the golden rules of good organization management is that every post should be defined by means of a job description – a formal statement of the purpose, duties and relationships of the job. Clearly, those delegated tasks and responsibilities which, in sum, form the 'core functions' of a post should be outlined within the job description – for, after all, that is what the document is all about. With all this in mind, tackle the following:

1 Firstly, the sixty-four-thousand-dollar question – are there actually job descriptions in existence for each of your subordinates?

If so –

a Er, when did the file copies last see the light of day?

b When were they last up-dated to take account of the ever-changing facets of any job?

c More particularly, do the job descriptions include those delegated tasks which – originally of an occasional, even 'one-off' nature – are now, with the passage of time, regular and significant features of the posts?

d And when did you last discuss the pros and cons of amending the job descriptions with those most concerned, the poor old job-holders themselves?

If there are no job descriptions in existence –

a Why the devil not? Is it because you consider such pieces of paper to be so much bumph, and a complete waste of time?

b If your direct span of control embraces more than, say, a couple of people, do you actually have the consummate cheek to assume that your brain can encompass, remember in every detail and regularly up-date a series of 'mental' job descriptions?

c And what about those subordinates, are they not entitled to have a formal statement of what they are supposed to do? Or do you feel that job descriptions would limit your beautiful freedom to change things at your whim?

You wretch. . . . Read no further until you have carried out one of the most basic (and important) functions of management; namely, placing everyone, including yourself, fully and accurately in the picture by producing job descriptions. You will likely be amazed at the anomalies that will be thrown up by such an exercise – and it will be well worth while on that score, alone.

2 Assuming that job descriptions are in existence, and are fully up-dated – what about 'cross-comparing' those delegated tasks? Would things dovetail more efficiently, and to everyone's greater satisfaction, if you reallocated sundry bits and pieces? It is only rarely that such a reappraisal fails to pay dividends. In other words, *think delegation* on an integrated, corporate scale – for that is the key to efficiency.

Notes on exercise nit-pick

Compare your scribbled notes with the following comments – remembering that the object of the game is to provide food for thought.

1 The extrovert manager is particularly keen on coming out with this much-vaunted remark – and, as a general statement of principle, it has some validity. If, however, it means that the odd manager-proponent spends bags of valuable time immersing himself in the finest nitty-gritty of a subordinate's tasks (merely to prove the truth of the statement), then it is not so good. Is it strictly necessary, say, that the production manager should know the precise ins-and-outs of every machine process handled by his workers – when, perhaps, with a production foreman and maintenance supervisor working under him, the operatives are not even within his direct span of control? Consider your own set-up, reader – and think on't.

2 I would hope that you had no hesitation in condemning this one – for one of the prime advantages of delegation is the very fact that, administered fairly and well, the process does induce a healthy and much-required sense of importance in subordinates. Thank goodness it does, for such a feeling leads to that golden asset, pride in one's work – and that is not a prerogative of management alone.

3 There is a world of difference between 'apparent logic' and the true stuff. In any event, this excuse (and that is precisely what it is) for failing to delegate is quite unforgivable – so never, ever let it be your war-cry.

4 A bit woolly – but, in essence, since we know that the manager who delegates adequately will thereby have more time for the primary function of 'managing', it must follow that maximization of the latter activity can be a step on the way to enhancing prospects of promotion. Of course, it is also necessary that the 'managing' is of acceptable quality. . . .

5 A short and sharp reaction – entirely and inescapably true. The next chapter will have a bit to say on this topic, so bide your time.

6 Arrant rubbish. To make subordinates totally responsible for delegated tasks is to abdicate one's position as manager – the buck of ultimate responsibility passes steadily and inevitably upwards in any organization.

7 A seeming red herring? Think about it – in terms of 'managing' and 'operating' functions, and the answer becomes clear.

8 If you believe this mad statement to be true, you had better go back to the start of this chapter – or, better still, resign.

It is high time we moved on to a consideration of the component aspects of delegation – so, having rounded off our look at delegators' ills, let us do exactly that.

4 Getting down to the nitty-gritty

> There are people whom one should like very well to drop, but would not wish to be dropped by.
>
> Dr Samuel Johnson
> Boswell's *Life of Johnson*

Since delegation is, in essence, the assignment of authority and responsibility to another person for the purpose of carrying out specific activities, it is plainly necessary that we should remind ourselves exactly what it is that we hand out to Jane and Willy Subordinate – and we can aptly summarize it thus:

AUTHORITY	is	POWER
RESPONSIBILITY	is	ACCOUNTABILITY

One means of illustrating these all-important terms is to take (very nicely and with the best of intentions) the evergreen example of the civil servant. By way of relevant anecdote, when Bob Trotter, an unwilling conscript to the army of those without work, visits his local Social Security office for the first time, he will likely be informed of a positive plethora of 'supplementary benefits' – to which he may (or, more probably, may not) be entitled. Let us assume that in his innocence Bob opts for a certain allowance – only to be told in round terms by the somewhat harassed official behind the counter, 'No, sorry – the fact that you've sixteen dogs and a parrot to feed doesn't entitle you to any more money.' Now, it may well be that Bob is slightly put out by this reaction, and, leaning both hands on the counter, he proceeds to expand on the fact that dog biscuits and parrot food are expensive – only to be told abruptly that clause 1132, sub-para (c) of the regulations prohibits dogs and parrots being fed on the State.

The point of this sad saga is, the civil servant concerned (a very junior cog in a very big machine) has wielded *enormous authority* in so rejecting Bob's claim; the 'it's in the book' reason exemplifies the junior official's use of nothing less than the power and majesty of the law – and, despite what our imaginary Trotter may think, rightly so too. But what of this self-same individual's *levels of responsibility*? They pale into relative insignificance when expressed, as they have to be, in terms of actual accountability – for if this were not so, all junior-grade civil servants would require to be paid on the same scale as cabinet ministers and judges.

Clearly, our basic definitions must be expanded:

AUTHORITY is POWER   *But only sufficient (never more) to enable the delegate to perform the required task.*

(Apropos our example, all civil servants wield very hefty authority in relation to their oft-junior status.)

RESPONSIBILITY   *But only sufficient (never total) to make the delegate*
is ACCOUNTABILITY   *liable to account for his success or failure in carrying out the task concerned.*

(While I would not wish to denigrate the civil servant's job, his or her levels of accountability – if only in terms of the penalties involved – are minimal in comparison with business and industry in general. Lest you doubt this, remember that the 'it's in the book' dictum provides a truly magnificent protective shield.)

For any delegation to be effective, *fully adequate* levels of authority and responsibility must be allocated – no more, no less.

Let us pursue this theme a mite further. When, say, a reliable cleaner is instructed (delegated) by his foreman to sweep a certain floor, the task is simple enough and the subordinate sufficiently trustworthy for the vital prerequisites of authority and responsibility to be merely implied:

'George, get the hall floor swept next, please.'

George knows that if anyone happens to challenge him while sweeping the hall, he is happily placed authority-wise, and won't hesitate to say as much:

'Don't go on at me, Mr Brown – if you've got any queries, take 'em up with the boss.'

George also knows that if he makes a bad job of the sweeping, the foreman will have his hide, and no mistake. But, leaving this second example aside, if the task to be delegated is of a more complicated nature, then the levels of authority and responsibilty must be spelled out – always taking into account, of course, such factors as the rapport which exists between the manager and the subordinate concerned, the knowledge and experience of the latter, and the quality of his or her motivation to succeed. Consider the following:

'John, I'm afraid I've got another chore for you which has to be done this afternoon. It's concerning the Routledge order. . . . I've just heard that the damned printers have let us down – despite their promise, they can't get those

APROPOS OF SOMETHING No. 4

Every now and again, the British government (in common with all other governments) dreams up a new, country-saving scheme – and, in order to put whatever it is into effect, creates yet another organization. In the UK, the Manpower Services Commission is a typical example of what I mean. One major MSC role, claimed by those in the Whitehall corridors of power to be innovative *and* country-saving, is the Youth Training Scheme – whereby, in essence, the disgracefully massive figure of young unemployed is shrouded by the youngsters concerned being allocated to employers (who obtain their labour for virtually nothing), plus the provision of some feverish 'further education' at colleges, for a period of twelve months. The success of the YTS plainly depends on the ability of the lower echelons of the MSC to persuade and convince employers that these young people are worthy (as undoubtedly the majority of them are) of being taken on as full-time employees. So, the MSC top brass were faced with delegating a vital task which, for effective implementation, required – and still so requires – a very high degree of personal determination and enthusiasm in each and every subordinate at the sharp end.

So far so good – or is it? While the MSC has been extremely lucky (and I use that term advisedly, for their selection skills in general do not exactly shine as paragons of assessment virtue) in recruiting a fairly large number of truly dedicated officials at local level, it is an undeniable fact that far too many of these junior and middle-level managers are narrow-minded apologies for the missionaries they are supposed, and required, to be.

At the risk of upsetting individual apple-carts and being accused of knocking the MSC, I offer that it's the old, old story – and it doesn't only apply to government departments. When top management decides to implement an innovative project, one which relies for success on continuing motivation of the highest order, *they* are nearly always suitably imbued with enthusiasm, determination and so on –but, as the nitty-gritty of the project is delegated steadily downwards and finally comes to rest on the shoulders of the actual 'doers', these essential qualities become hopelessly diluted. In other words, *at the level where it matters*, that which at the outset was innovative (maybe even revolutionary) in concept is presented and accepted as 'just another job' – and, as a result, the original spirit and intent of the thing is liable to be knocked for six.

When and if you have occasion to delegate, do *you* take this diminution of enthusiasm, dedication (etc.) into full account, *and do something about it?*

specifications run off until next week, at the earliest. I want you to see if you can persuade Mick Rawlings to do the job for us. Give him my compliments and explain the urgency of the situation. You'll need all those figures you got out the other day – go through 'em with Rawlings and put him fully in the picture. . . . Remember to let me know how you get on – I'll be back in the office by about three-thirty. . . .'

Assuming a good working relationship between John and his manager, the boss has done a satisfactory job of allocating authority and responsibility:

Authority

'I've got another chore for you'
'Give him my compliments and explain'

Responsibility

'Remember to let me know how you get on'

Now consider this next example:

'Right, Hawkins, what's next . . .? Yes, I think it would be best if you concentrated on the two Fords in Bays 3 and 9 – they've both been promised for 4.30. See Fred Carruthers and tell him from me that the cleaners will have to be finished within the next hour, otherwise you'll never get finished in time. Let me know as soon as you've completed both jobs, please. . . . Remember, four-thirty's the deadline . . . .'

There is a slightly different working relationship here. The allocation of authority and responsibility is far more explicit:

Authority

'. . . if you concentrated on . . .'
'See Fred Carruthers and tell him from me'

Responsibility

'Let me know as soon as you've completed both jobs'
'Remember, four-thirty's the deadline'

Perhaps the classic example of an absolutely definitive allocation of authority and responsibility is to be found in the composition of a military operations order – which average format, albeit far too detailed for adoption by business and industry, certainly presses home the need for full attention to be paid to this vital prerequisite of effective delegation. Lives may not literally depend on the successful outcome of Bertie Blogg's delegation of work to his staff – but it is no exaggeration to say that the very livelihood of all those concerned can be affected by any fall-down on his part in allocating levels of authority and responsibility.

The beastly span of control

In times of economic recession, while governments occupy themselves with talk of silver linings and pleas that the national belt be pulled even tighter, employers have little choice but to prune their strained resources – and, as many of us know to our cost, redundancy rears its ugly head. Unfortunately and just in passing, many employers take the thing a stage further and use 'the recession' as a handy excuse to savagely trim their management teams – secure in the knowledge that those executives who escape the swinging axe will be willing to accept almost any workload in preference to sudden and prolonged unemployment. Be that as it may, even the fair-minded organization finding itself in straitened economic circumstances is normally forced to reduce its management strength – with the inevitable result that individual spans of control take a mighty beating.

A manager's span of control, the number of employees reporting *directly* to a particular executive, will plainly affect the quantity and quality of delegated work – if only for the reason that, as the span widens, it becomes increasingly difficult for the manager to monitor results. Thus, at the very time when the overworked guy or gal should be delegating more work to subordinates, the circumstances of the situation dictate that such essential action will be rendered almost completely ineffective. If things are further complicated by the pressures of an unfeeling and coercive top management, who refuse even to acknowledge that members of their team (and the efficiency of their outfit) can suffer in such circumstances – then, of course, the overall outcome can be fatal.

As if that were not enough, there are not even any straws at which the overworked executive can clutch in terms of arguing, if he so dares, a case for a reduced span of control. Any limit on the number of people reporting directly to a manager is determined, not by the application of a golden rule, but purely and simply by the factors which may or may not apply in each specific case. These could include:

a   the personal competence of the manager;

b   the nature of the overall job of the bailiwick, and the component tasks of the staff concerned;

c   questions of time available;

d   the geographical location of all concerned – i.e. communication problems;

e   the quality, in terms of experience and competence, of the sub-ordinates.

So, in a sad nutshell, the manager who wishes to argue for a reduced span of control will likely be forced to stand or fall by his or her personal powers of persuasion – but, for all that, those who find themselves in such adverse circumstances must take up the cudgel, or face the almost certain prospect of much worse to come.

Co-ordinated delegation

In the last self-tutorial the section headed 'A touch of organization' referred among other things to the need for 'cross-comparing' delegated tasks:

- Are you thinking of delegating a task to Mary which, in fact, has features in common with something currently being actioned by Bill – indicating, just perhaps, that the two activities should be combined, and implemented by one of them?

- While such a similarity may not have existed when the tasks were originally delegated, have the changes wrought by time and events produced exactly that – unknown to you, their manager?

- In delegating tasks, have you taken accurate account of varying personal strengths and weaknesses in your staff – and, if not, isn't it time that a redistribution of activities took place?

- Who is the Cinderella of your staff – that poor unfortunate who, for whatever reason, is starved of delegated tasks? What are you going to do about a situation which is clearly your responsibility to resolve?

The vital question of 'what' to delegate

At this point it would be very easy to merely repeat that, in deciding exactly what jobs are to be delegated, a manager should hive off as many of his 'operating' tasks as possible – and leave it at that. Well, we are not going to. Like it or not, there are some additional and very important considerations to be taken into account.

The essential audit   Any manager worthy of the name will not be content with maintaining a broad-brush, mental picture of his or her subordinates' skills and experience – for, given a staff of more than two or three (coupled with the frailties of the human mind), the average executive is incapable of assimilating, accurately remembering and placing into use even a fraction of the required information. No, using facts and indications derived from such sources as the periodic appraisal or development interviews, the outcome of specific instances of delegation, the evidence of the manager's own eyes (to name but a few), the wise boss will compile a 'staff resources diary' – call it what you will – in which will be recorded regularly up-dated information on individual strengths and weaknesses. Then and only then will the manager be in a viable position to commence a programme of really effective delegation. All right, what happens then?

Allocating to each his own   Each task to be delegated should be carefully examined and, metaphorically speaking, tagged:

- What skills are required, and at what levels?

- What is the priority for completion?

The tasks should then be allocated to individuals, but always taking into account the following criteria:

- For high-priority tasks, allocation to the person most suited in terms of experience and proficiency.

- For tasks in which time is not of the essence (and there are always a goodly number of these), allocation as often as possible to those people who, lacking experience and even proficiency, NEED to perform such work to bring them up to standard. If training is required, then training should be given.

This apparently simple dictum is perhaps the most heartily ignored of all basic principles of man management – *delegation does not merely exist for the purpose of getting work done – it is the prime process by which a manager's staff are exercised and developed to the sensible limits of individual capability and potential.* And, reader, believe otherwise at your peril.

Again, it's on to the self-tutorial with flags flying –and determination oozing from every pore. . . .

Self-tutorial

A pause for thought

Before plunging into an exercise it might be a good idea, as it were, to draw the strings together – and consider a number of the main points we have covered thus far. Have a good look at Figure 2. Lest you succumb to the feeling that the diagram does little other than highlight the obvious, ask yourself one simple question: *if* things are so blatantly obvious, why is it that so many managers fail to delegate wisely and well?

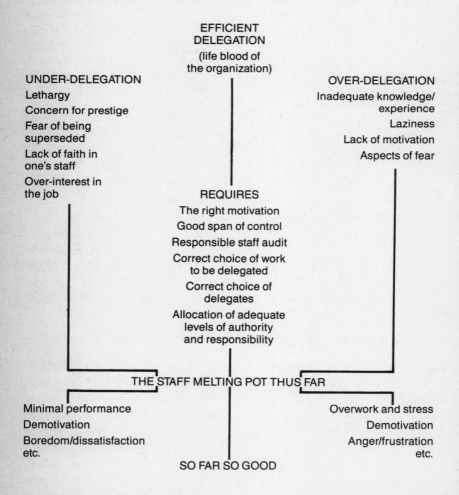

Figure 2   *A reminder of salient points*

Validating a task for delegation

Imagine that you are considering the delegation of a certain task to one of your subordinates. Clearly, being a manager of some calibre, you wish to ensure:

a   that the activity concerned is, indeed, one which should be so delegated:

   and

b   that you allocate it to the member of staff most suited to carry it out.

How would you ensure that these criteria are satisfied? Without sneaking a look at past pages, have a shot at compiling a detailed check-list of the points you would take into consideration. Then, following our usual drill, place your answer on one side for comparison with the notes at the end of this self-tutorial.

A question of power and accountability

Here is a very simple little exercise that, who knows, may even be beneath your contempt. So, be a devil – prove that you are clearly above such basic things by answering it. What are the penalties faced by the delegator who fails to allocate correct levels of authority and responsibility? That's right, consult your detailed notes. . . .

And a bit more on span of control

In the preceding chapter, I listed the five main factors which can influence a manager's effective span of control – and, hence, cast an ominous shadow over the efficacy of his delegation. Test your memory by listing them, and then proceed to demonstrate your understanding of these vital factors by enlarging on the implications involved. Once again, we will compare notes in a minute.

Notes on validating a task for delegation

Suffice it to say that your answer should embrace something along the following lines:

Point a
1   The all-important question. . . . Looking at your personal slop-chit, does the job concerned fall safely under the 'operating' heading – or is it a 'managing' activity, which should not be delegated?

2   Assuming that it is an 'operating' activity, are you satisfied that you have taken all the ramifications of the task into account? In essence, is it sufficiently self-contained – or are there possible factors (side-issues,

'knock-on' effects, etc.) which could inhibit the delegatee's successful implementation of your instructions?

Point b

1 Considerations of technical know-how and experience apart, does the task demand the application of any important peripheral abilities, for example:

- A better-than-average, perhaps innate skill at dealing with people?

- Particular patience, or skill at attending to minute detail?

- Especially good powers of written communication?

And so on.

2 Bearing in mind the priority of the task, who among your staff is either *best qualified* OR *best suited in terms of gaining valuable experience* to undertake the activity? If relevant, does this person possess the necessary peripheral abilities, or is an amended choice indicated?

3 Will the chosen member of staff be able to absorb the delegated task without undue difficulty, or is some adjustment of his/her workload required?

4 Does the proposed task fall in line with the established duties and responsibilities of the person concerned – and, if not, is there a good case (other than sheer expediency) for the hapless individual to be thus clobbered? While it may sound cast-iron to you, would the case withstand the test of impartial inspection?

Well, did we manage to achieve at least some degree of unanimity with our notes? I certainly hope so – but, repeating myself *ad nauseum*, the main object of the game is to trigger your thoughts, and this exercise should have achieved that, if nothing else.

Notes on a question of power and accountability

Straightforward answers to a straightforward question:

Excessive authority

- Erosion of the manager's personal authority, with consequent loss of control.

- *'Power tends to corrupt, and absolute power corrupts absolutely.'* In my view when it comes to summing-up the second danger of allocating excessive authority to subordinates, Lord Acton's famous words cannot be bettered.

Inadequate authority
- Stress and frustration on the part of the subordinate concerned.

- Loss of respect – or, more likely, actual contempt – for the manager concerned.

- Partial or complete failure of the task.

Excessive responsibility
- Anxiety, stress and a totally unfair burden for the subordinate.

- Abrogation by the manager of *his* responsibility, with consequent loss of effective control – and contempt for his failure.

- Possible partial or complete failure of the task.

Inadequate responsibility
- Failure of the manager's function and dereliction of his duties to the delegatee, in that the latter's personal accountability for success or failure is seriously eroded.

- Being aware that full accountability is not thus required, the subordinate may well skimp or otherwise sabotage the task. In any event, inadequate responsibility spells a diminished challenge, and can only result in lowered morale and motivation to succeed.

APROPOS OF SOMETHING No. 6

In delegation, if everything appears to be going well, you have obviously overlooked something.

Notes on span of control

It is quite likely that far too many executives are saddled with excessive spans of control, and it does behove us to think seriously about the factors which can adversely affect this vital aspect of management. Again, see how your notes compare with the following points:

The personal competence of the manager This factor not only embraces questions of technical and general management know-how, but is also bound up with that all-important aspect, the personality of the manager

71

concerned. To quote but one example, some managers (dare it be said, too few?) are blessed with the innate ability to 'get on well' with others, especially their subordinates – and by that I do not mean sucking-up to juniors. Such lucky folk will often be able to cope with a wider span of control than their less fortunate colleagues. Personal inhibitions can and do spell serious trouble. . . .

The nature of the job   Plainly, the ability to maintain an effective span of control is directly proportional to the overall nature and complications of the job concerned. Sadly, this aspect is frequently overlooked when those at the helm dole out managers' responsibilities – they call it over-delegation.

The time available   Time is the manager's biggest enemy, and the battle most frequently lost. When, as is almost always the case, hours and minutes are at a premium, the span of effective control is bound to be seriously eroded. Flap decisions and inadequate attention to detail are the concomitants of many a management disaster – are they not?

The geographical location of staff   As all military strategists are aware, stretched lines of communication can be the harbingers of defeat, and the principle is no less true when applied to a manager's span of control. It is for this obvious but oft-ignored reason that many office-based sales managers and other controllers of dispersed personnel are inhibited in their striving for overall efficiency – and why, as a consequence, so much time is taken up with those dreaded 'all into the office for the day' meetings. Needless to say, even the department which happens to be located on, say, two floors can present problems to the person in charge – and adversely affect his or her span of control.

The experience and competence of subordinates   Another very obvious factor – but one which, again, is frequently overlooked. While it may be directly attributable to a manager's shortcomings as a 'trainer and developer of staff' that undue time has to be expended on steering and controlling, this does not negate the fact that the span of control will suffer – thereby triggering a vicious circle of inefficiency.

That concludes our examination of the mechanical bits and pieces which comprise the delegation process, and we now have to take a long, hard look at another vital consideration; the quality of the fuel which, injected into the machine, determines its ultimate performance – in other words, the intensely personal business of communicating one's delegation require-ments to the lads and lassies at the sharp, doing end.

5 The gentle art of dishing it out

I am not arguing with you – I am telling you.

J.A. McNeill Whistler
The Gentle Art of Making Enemies

One piece of management lingo which is a firm favourite of those who pontificate on the subject is the term 'organization climate'. For all that it is pure jargon, the words do aptly describe one of the most important syndromes that, staring every executive in the face, provides a rock-solid, on-going indication of just how good Jack or Jill Manager is at controlling people. Defined as the state of employee relations prevailing at any one time within an outfit, the organization climate and its constant fluctuations are plainly of vital significance to the would-be delegator.*

Unfortunately, when a certain breed of manager is reminded just how essential it is to preserve an equable organization climate, the likely reaction is one of some scorn:

Look, I'm in this business to make a profit – not feather-bed a motley crowd of layabouts. . . .'

'Yes, all right – but the point is, I just haven't got the time to spend on all this psychological stuff.'

It is something of an irony that these self-same managers are usually the first to protest that their employees 'have gone all bolshie' as the result of some directive or imposed condition of work. Conveniently overlooking the fact that it takes two to tango, such scallywag executives tend to rest on their blight-ridden laurels – often to the point where the entire workforce is regarded as nothing less than the enemy within:

'Frankly, I'm fed-up to the teeth with do-gooders telling me that I'm to blame for the way things are. . . . If you had the kind of lazy, uninterested bunch that I'm saddled with, if you had to contend with shop stewards who're interested in

---

* For the purposes of this chapter, an 'organization' can be of any size, ranging from those two people in the outer office to the massive, corporate spread of a multinational giant – for the simple reason that when two or more employees are slung together, there is, inevitably, a 'climate'.

nothing but stirring-up trouble – well, you'd know exactly what I mean. The whole bloody industry is falling apart – and, I tell you, if this money-grubbing, pig-ignorant shower don't come to their senses pretty soon, there'll be nothing left for 'em to moan about. So, as I say, don't talk to me about organization climate and all that claptrap. . . . Go and spread your gospel where it matters, down there on the shop-floor – not that it'll do an iota of good. . . .'
(*A production manager who got pretty hot under the white collar during a seminar on negotiation tactics.*)

Thank goodness, this is neither the time nor the place in which to launch a barrage of comments and advice on industrial relations – but, having said that, it would be totally unrealistic even to envisage the delegation process without giving a whole lot of thought to the basic question of organization climate. Also, as you may recall, the introductory chapter dwelt on the intensely personal business of management style – the adoption, wilfully or otherwise, by an executive of an autocratic, democratic, consultative (etc.)

APROPOS OF SOMETHING No. 7

As I write, the merciless jaws of recession continue to gnaw at the vitals of organizations at home and abroad – and, very sadly, this worrying state of affairs has caused many managers to undergo sinister changes of attitude and style. Not once but umpteen times in recent months I've come across instances of executives who, previously moderate and participative in their management approach, have become quite different animals – and nowhere has this been more pronounced than in the area of motivation. Dealing as I do with a succession of management students, I've received tragically constant reports of bosses (mostly overworked and worried for their own security) who have resorted to such motivational horrors as:

'Look, m'lad, just do it – you want to keep your job, don't you?'

'Remember, there's plenty of 'em out there – just dying to get into your shoes. . . .'

Although it will probably weigh little in the minds of the managers who have thus changed their spots, it is relevant to note that subordinates have long memories – and, when times improve and the self-same bosses are only too happy to revert to their former selves, they may wonder why they are not once again top o'the pops. . . .

They will also discover the unpleasant truth in the adage: '*It's a manager's subordinates who bring about his death, not his superiors.*'

---

role in dealing with subordinates. Whichever comes first in this chicken-and-egg situation, an inbred management personality or that which is shaped and determined by the attitudes of others, is immaterial – in terms of delegation, it is the end-result that matters (see Figure 3).

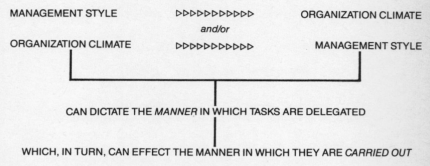

Figure 3   *Management style and organization climate*

So it is necessary to consider the manner in which tasks are delegated. . . . Spelling this next topic out, it means quite simply that the mere ordering of something to be done, however well-salted with an adequate allocation of authority and responsibility, is just not sufficient – for, with the possible exception of the armed services and other, similarly disciplined organizations (and the absence of an emergency in our workaday world), one's subordinates require and deserve two further ingredients for the recipe to meet with success:

●   They must be *motivated* to succeed. The important business of putting juniors fully in the picture when tasks are handed out is not, as some managers would have it, a form of toadying to the workers. It is the sure-fire method by which every thinking boss stirs a subordinate into rising to the challenge of a job, thereby instilling a belief that only his or her best efforts will suffice. If, by virtue of the absolute simplicity of a task, it is impracticable or, as may well be the case, impossible to provide this desired background detail, then it should be remembered that the delegator's overall manner when directing a junior can, in itself, convey unmistakable 'motivational overtones'. Consider, for example, the effects of varying tone and emphasis in the following, simple act of delegation:

'John, let me have a full report on the Maddox order as soon as possible, please. I'm seeing 'em tomorrow morning.'
(Expressed in a pleasantly even tone of voice, conveying a clear implication of faith in John's ability to come up with the goods. This is hard to describe in cold print, but I'm sure you know what I mean.)

As opposed to –

'John, let me have a FULL REPORT on the Maddox order AS SOON AS POSSIBLE, please. I'm seeing 'em TOMORROW MORNING.'
(The motivational bit has certainly changed in character and import – to the extent that it could convey a threatened kick in the direction of John's [implied] lazy posterior.)

Or, for instance –

'John, let ME have a full report on the Maddox order as soon as possible, please. I'M seeing 'em tomorrow morning.'
(Expressed in a certain tone, the directive could now be a demotivator – in that John has received a clear indication that he is not considered sufficiently capable to deal with the matter himself.)

- There must be the opportunity for *consultation* in all but the most minor acts of delegation. The subordinate who is denied the chance to inject his often valuable comments or suggestions regarding a delegated task will rapidly become frustrated – and, of course, the dictator-manager who insists on such a unilateral approach cannot but lose out sooner or later. There is, however, a stern caveat to this business of encouraging consultation. Consider the following, albeit simplistic, example:

'Jean, I'd like you to interview this next candidate – unless, of course, you'd rather not.'

This particular 'opportunity to consult' is, in fact, an open invitation for Jean to duck the issue, and provides a solid indication that the manager concerned is unsure of himself – and his subordinate. Consider one alternative and, you may think, more suitably couched version:

'Jean, I'd like you to interview this next candidate. Now, tell me, d'you have any queries – is there any way in which I can help?'

We have arrived at the point, then, where it is necessary to accept that the handing-out of a delegated task, the actual format of the verbal or written instructions, must consist whenever possible of four component parts:

First element	The 'action' or 'stirring' bit – the instruction itself. A vital sub-component of this first element is the necessity to make the *objective* of the task crystal-clear – a crucial point which, for some reason or other, is commonly overlooked by managers. Putting it bluntly, an order without an objective is a sheer waste of time, and an offence against the basic principles of good management. Needless to say, the instruction must also include the requisite authority to perform the task.
Second element	The 'allocation' bit – the obvious fact that the subordinate is not only required to perform the given task,

but will also be held accountable for its completion. I've said it
before, but I intend to say it again: this does NOT mean
passing the buck of total responsibility to the junior
concerned – for that constitutes nothing less than pure
management abdication.

Third element   The 'motivation' bit – fanning that fire in the belly.

Fourth element   The 'consultation' bit – taking all advantage of the
undoubted wisdom of those at the sharp, *doing* end of
the manager's shebang.

But what about priorities?

Yes, indeed – work priorities must be considered. One common pitfall
encountered by executives who are anxiously striving to rid themselves of
the routine, 'doing' minutiae of their jobs is this vexed business of attaching
priorities to tasks – in that all but the screaming emergency assignments are
dished out with precious little attention being given to the order in which
they should be tackled. I will scramble further out on this particular limb,
and add that far too many of us tend to overlook our *personal* work priorities,
let alone those of our juniors. For instance, reader, when first you cast your
bleary, management-tired eyes over that bulging in-tray, exactly how often
do you actually sort the contents into a new pile of descending (oh, all right,
or ascending) work priorities? Be honest, now, and admit that a more likely
approach is to do a swift flurry through all those files and extract the odd,
really hot potato for emergency treatment – leaving the remainder more or
less in the same order as they were plonked there in the first place. No? Full
marks to you, thou true and faithful servant. . . .

Consider, if you will, the 'two-prong approach' to the allocation of
priorities in delegation, as outlined in Figure 4. Having dealt with the initial
questions of allocating priorities to all one's 'managing' tasks – and, lest we
forget, to the few, essential 'operating' tasks which cannot be delegated – it is
then necessary to consider *two* factors where one's subordinates are
concerned:

a   The 'work priority' of each task for delegation;

b   The 'staff allocation' priority in each case – i.e. who, of all the available
people, is best suited to (or best merits) each task?

Plainly, individual situations will play a large part in dictating the very
necessary refinements to the 'bare-bones' set-up depicted in Figure 4, but at
least the diagram does provide the all-important trigger for your own
thoughts on the subject of priorities in delegation. There will be more on
this particular aspect in the self-tutorial – when, dare I say it, you will be
working at it yourself. . . .

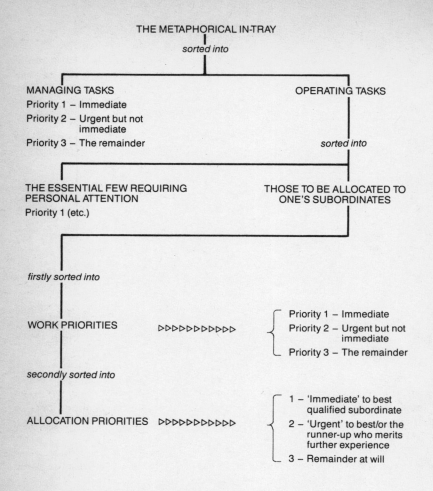

Figure 4   *A basic approach to the allocation of priorities*

Staff shortages

As I have intimated earlier in these pages, one pretty awful product of a recession is the necessity (or, in some wholly scurrilous cases, the temptation) for employers to cut costs by making numbers of their managers redundant – with the almost inevitable consequence that the survivors end up grossly overloaded with work. But it doesn't stop there, does it? One's subordinates, the people that really matter, also get the chop – and, in this case, the almost inevitable consequence is that you and I, as manager-survivors, grossly overload *their* hapless shoulders. Ah, yes, I can hear your spluttered defence:

> 'But, crikey, what can I do about it? I'd no option but to make some of them redundant – and those that remain just have to soldier on and get the work done, or we'll all end up on the breadline. . . . So don't make me out to be the wretched villain in the piece, because I'm not – I just have to do what I'm told. . . .'

Huh, if you will pardon the expression, in a pig's ear, you do. . . . It may read like one of those ridiculously pompous, totally unrealistic statements to which management authors, squatting comfortably in their ivory towers, are hellishly prone – but the cold fact is, *you have elected to become a manager, and you must act like a manager, OR GET OUT.* I am acutely aware that in urging you to do something about subordinates who are grossly overworked, such rocking the boat could mean that your own job is placed firmly on the line – and that, faced with that contingency, the average manager will definitely choose discretion in favour of valour. But, for all that, it has to be said. . . . One of the functions for which you are paid is to manage and stick up for the interests of *your* people. This takes nothing less than sterling courage. Do you have it?

If, as I suspect, you are not overkeen to bat against the law of the work jungle and fight to the death on behalf of your staff – well, are you absolutely confident that you have done everything short of making such a courageous stand? For example, have you:

1   completed a detailed review of all delegated jobs, checking their current validity (many tasks tend to outlast their original purpose and become thoroughly obsolescent), and pruning where humanly possible?

2   compared individual workloads, one with another, right across the board – and rectified the anomalies that certainly exist?

3   consulted with your subordinates – seriously considering their ideas and putting any good ones into practice?

So when are you going to start?

Shortcomings in staff

One truism of the employment game is that, like managers, there is no such thing as a perfect workforce. A further and far more cogent truism is that very few employees, managers included, receive the benefit of optimum training and encouragement to give of their best – and the buck for this failure sits solidly on the desks of the seniors concerned. Perhaps the lip-service paid by the vast majority of executives to employee development and training would appear less reprehensible if (and here is a hollow thought) it was not accompanied by the ceaseless moan about staff clangers and shortcomings – for the two make illogical and unacceptable bed-fellows.

As one who has been associated with training on and off for many years, I get heartily sick of meeting those umpteen, complacent managers who, just because they have one subordinate attending some part-time day release course or other, regard themselves as with-it, on-the-ball developers of staff. This common inability to see the training wood for the trees is, of course, another root cause of delegated tasks ending up in partial or total failure. It is simply no good gaily dishing out work if those on the receiving end have been inadequately trained to carry it out; and woe betide the rogue manager who thinks that delegating someone to sit by Nellie will conveniently solve the problem. It won't. Here is one good reason why Figure 4 is labelled 'A *basic* approach to the allocation of priorities' – for the process of handing out jobs must always be prefaced by a review of the capabilities required, and action taken to remedy the weaknesses which invariably will be revealed.

This chapter's self-tutorial is devoted to provoking your thoughts on the manner in which *you* delegate tasks – and, to be fairly blunt, it will require more than a touch of candour on your part. So play the game, do!

Self-tutorial

Exercise dish-it-out

Examine the following 'mini-scripts' and, making imaginative allowance for the limitations of such an exercise, jot down some notes on what you think of the approach to delegation revealed in each case.

MINI-SCRIPT 1

(*Manager to junior clerk*)   'Jill, we've simply got to do something about the state of this printout of mail-shot addresses. . . . I want you to go through them and whip out all the deadwood. I dare say that a good half of them are firms that closed down years ago. Get cracking on it as soon as you've finished whatever you're doing. . . .'

MINI-SCRIPT 2

(*Manager to assembled group of staff*)   'Let me get one thing straight. . . . Whether you like it or not, this job has got to be completed by Friday – and I mean Friday. I've described exactly what's required to be done, and there can be no possible excuse for anyone failing to meet the deadline . . . . (*Turns to supervisor*) 'Joe, you know the set-up – and, despite what you've told me, I'm quite certain that if everyone pulls their weight for a change, there won't be any snags. Perhaps you'd care to bear in mind that I'm looking to you as supervisor to ensure – just this once – that things go smoothly and according to plan. I don't think that's asking too much. . . .' (*Faces group*) 'Now, for goodness sake, let's get cracking.'

MINI-SCRIPT 3

(*Senior executive addressing his management team*)   'Your attention, please, ladies and gentlemen – the time's moving on, and I'm sure you wish to get back to your sections. I've outlined the overall aims of the campaign, and I'm more than confident that you'll do all within your power to ensure that they are achieved. Needless to say, the final outcome will be largely determined by your measure of success in taking this first, vital initiative – so give it everything you've got – and good luck to you all. . . .'

MINI-SCRIPT 4

(*Manager, responding to subordinate's comments*)   'Yes, Mary, I know the blessed job's not in line with what you've been doing up to now, but don't you see – you owe it to yourself to broaden your general experience, and here's a heaven-sent opportunity to do exactly that! You just leave it to me to worry about any snags, that's what I'm paid for. . . . All I want you to do is get out there and pitch into things – all right, m'dear?'

MINI-SCRIPT 5

(*You-know-who to his subordinates*)   'Right, you lot, when you've finished 'avin your little chinwag, come over 'ere – there's a job as needs doin' to this 'ere pile. . . . D'yer hear me, you 'orrible bleeders? Right, then – move yer flipping' selves!'

MINI-SCRIPT 6

(*Manager addressing his team*)   'Well, there we are. . . . I know it's a damned awful job, but there's no option – we've just got to get stuck into it. . . . Otherwise, they'll be down on our necks like a ton of bricks – and that's the last thing we want, isn't it?'

Bearing in mind that we are presently concerned with the communicative aspects of delegation (and, as I have already intimated, that any written exercise of this nature will always smack of something larger than life), let us compare notes.

Mini-script 1   If this was all that the manager had to say to his junior clerk, it is to be hoped that the young employee was equipped with the necessary knowledge and experience to carry out the task – for she certainly received little in the way of guidance from her boss. If, however, there is an indictment nestling between the lines of this quote, it is almost certainly the manager's lack of interest in Jill's current work. For all he knew or cared, the poor lass could have been up to her neck with some complicated activity or other – and, as a consequence, thrown into quite a tizzy as a result of this further and unthinking lump of delegation. Last but by no means least, the word 'please' and the odd pleasantry would not have gone amiss. As I am sure you are aware, subordinates (and *especially* youngsters) thrive on concrete evidence that the boss, whatever his or her other failings, is capable of the common niceties in life – which they require and deserve.

Mini-script 2   Unless you, reader, are archetypal of the many sour-minded and surly executives that still infest the woodwork of far too many offices (which, of course, you are not), I am sure you will agree that the quote reflects a pretty ropey organization climate – and a lousy manager, to boot. Whatever preceded this approach in terms of staff fall-downs and attitudes, there can be no excuse whatsoever for such a public and highly sarcastic attack on a supervisor. As the old adage reminds us, there is a time and place for everything – and this was certainly not it. Delegation communicated in this manner amounts to little short of a capital offence.

Mini-script 3   Fairly obviously, a peroration by an executive big-wig who, for my money, has acquitted himself well in thus bringing things to a close. Perhaps the only ingredient missing in this commendable mix is a final 'Any last questions?'

Mini-script 4   Although we cannot accurately assess this executive's comments in the context of what went on beforehand, there is more than a hint to the effect that Mary has protested her inability to carry out the task concerned – and that the boss is blandishing his way through her objections. Assuming that this is so, he stands very little chance of motivating Mary to do other than feel contempt for his unthinking and ill-qualified stab at delegation.

Mini-script 5   Not exactly the textbook manager-type image, eh? But just in case you dismissed this little quote as an irrelevant, cartoon-type picture of an army corporal dealing with his charges, remember that there are managers of this ilk – and, of their number, a blessed few have subordinates who would willingly walk on water if so ordered. One of the finest managers I have ever known was just such a rough-cut diamond who, albeit that he addressed everyone in mightily down-to-earth, salty terms (thereby upsetting the sensibilities of many of his 'more refined' peers and seniors every time he opened his mouth), enjoyed the undying respect of his staff. Boy, did he get results from that dedicated and hard-working team.

But, and here is the rub, the technique of successfully motivating subordinates by 'treating 'em rough', however refined a manager may be, cannot usually be learned. More often than not, it is a product of an innate and quite unique personality trait. The sobering message is, experiment at your peril.

Mini-script 6   A *manager* addressing his *team*? A likely story, indeed. . . . This cowardly, buck-passing approach fools no one, least of all any subordinates who are forced to endure such verbal slime. To make things worse, if that is possible, the rascal of a so-called manager has actually attempted to get his juniors to agree with his faintly nauseating attitude. Blaming 'the people upstairs' for the need to impose tasks on juniors is a favourite ploy of the weak-kneed, incompetent executive – who should not be allowed within a mile of any position of authority over others.

A personal checklist on the art of dishing it out

Sitting firmly in the privacy of your own conscience, see how you get on with the following questionnaire:

1   To what extent do I obey the 'four-component rule'

INSTRUCTING	–	detailing the task and giving the authority
ALLOCATING	–	detailing accountability
MOTIVATING	–	encouraging best effort
CONSULTING	–	seeking suggestions

when delegating all but the most trivial of tasks?

2   Before making my requirements known to whomever is concerned, how much solid thought do I give to the widely varying effects of

> COMMANDS
> INSTRUCTIONS
> REQUESTS
> SUGGESTIONS
> *and*
> DOWNRIGHT PLEAS

when thus dealing with staff?

Or, to put it another way, am I really so skilled at human relationships that I automatically come up with the 'right format for the right person' on each and every occasion? And how often do I anxiously resort to the downright plea, albeit that I know this to be a rank abdication of my management authority?

3   Inspecting myself through the eyes and ears of my subordinates, how does my general attitude *really* rate with them? Am I, just perhaps, regarded as

> ABRUPT
> STAND-OFFISH
> 'FLAT', DEVOID OF FEELING
> ILL AT EASE
> OVERBEARING
> DOGMATIC
> INDECISIVE

Or what?

4   And what reaction do I detect in my subordinates when I am handing out tasks – particularly when I look them in the eye? Is it generally one of

> INTEREST
> APATHY
> DISLIKE
> BOREDOM
> SCORN

Or what?

5   And whose fault is this?

6   How does my skill in delegating tasks compare with the performance of my colleagues?

7   And exactly what grounds do I have for thinking thus?

8   If my colleagues were asked to rate *me*, what would be the tenor of their assessments?

9 Hold on, have I tackled this questionnaire with absolute candour – or have I succumbed to the temptation of kidding myself?

10 If so, why?

I commend the last two questions to your earnest thought – since, far from being Smart Alec-type queries, they provide the key to the principal nasty in management's very own Pandora's Box. Put it this way, if this first-created woman of Greek mythology *was* responsible for letting loose all conceivable ills on the world, she must have had managers in mind when she unleashed the viper of self-deception – for most of us carry its venom in our veins. When, on those very rare occasions, we do sit back and consider our personal skills and performances, we tend to do so with practised self-deception – thinking little but nicely cosy thoughts, and basking in the warmth of our imagined proficiency.

If the cap fits. . . .

6 Keeping one's ear to the ground

Give every man thy ear. . . .

> William Shakespeare
> *Hamlet*, Act I, Scene iii

It would be really easy to dispose of this chapter's opening theme by resort to one of those holier-than-thou homilies so favoured by textbook authors – and if, perchance, I did elect for such a tempting way out, I would probably offer something like this:

'One secret of effective delegation is management awareness.'

Now, to be fair, no one can deny the absolute truth of this starchy assertion. The trouble is, it does precious little good for the poor old reader who, seeing the words, is left high and dry when it comes to doing something about it:

'Hum, management awareness. . . . What a bore – I wonder if dinner's ready yet?' *or* 'Oh, to hell with it – management awareness, indeed. . . . Why in blazes doesn't this guy get off his pedestal?'

Well, it is my intention to do exactly that – but, before we get cracking, I think it only fair to issue a kind of storm warning. In detailing this man's answer to the need for all delegators to develop 'management awareness', I will be thrusting a pretty big bone of contention down your reading gullet. So stand by to be suitably outraged.

In order to practise delegation with any degree of proficiency, a manager must acquire and constantly up-date an in-depth knowledge of his or her subordinates – and by this I mean a deal more than a continuing familiarity with their workplace strengths and weaknesses. Just as important (and here we get to the contentious bit) is an all-embracing knowledge of their individual lifestyles away from work – their domestic situations, personal foibles, troubles, hang-ups, and so on. In short, I am advocating that you drive a horse and cart through the generally accepted convention that an employee's private life is sacrosanct, and that you become a dyed-in-the-wool, all-nosey Paul Pry. *This*, if you like, is management awareness, and the very stuff on which effective delegation, and management in general, is founded – the nitty-gritty intelligence

APROPOS OF SOMETHING No. 9

A somewhat hairy and cautionary tale. . . .

A good manager-friend of mine recently went to town on this essential business of being an executive Paul Pry – and, shortly afterwards, sought me out in my favourite saloon bar. I could see by his face that he wasn't exactly brimming with joy, and it took no longer than the pulling of a pint to find out why. . . .

'Oh, goodness, yes – I've learned some interesting bits an' bobs, just as you said I would. . . . The trouble is, most of what I overheard was about *me* – and, I tell you, some of it came as a shock. . . .'

Now, I know that this particular chappie has the strength of character to sort out the wheat from the chaff of what he overheard, and the good old-fashioned common sense to do something about improving that which mattered.

Are you similarly equipped?

gathering which, in sum, provides the thinking executive with highly possible reasons why juniors tick and behave as they do:

- Perhaps WHY Mary could not restrain that slight grimace when she realized that a delegated activity would involve some overtime.

- Perhaps WHY Tom, when tackling a newly allocated task, did so with an uncharacteristic lack of care.

- Perhaps WHY, for no apparent reason, Anna-Jane shilly-shallied around, instead of getting to grips with a certain job.

- Perhaps WHY your supervisor, previously a person of great tact and efficiency, has started nagging at the staff of late.

- Perhaps WHY that young trainee has suddenly lost his sparkle and will to succeed.

And so on.

There is only one way to achieve this intimate knowledge, and that is by growing Dumbo-sized ears – and, ignoring one's sense of fair play, training them to *eavesdrop* on each and every word uttered by staff. Then, for instance, by dint of mental sorting and processing, the manager can link Mary's comment to George on Tuesday morning with her half-smothered exclamation during a telephone call on Thursday – and, if he is lucky, begin to form a picture of possibly why the lass is not quite her normal, equable self. I make no bones about this business of spying on one's subordinates; it is *not* cricket, and therefore will likely offend the reader who entertains firm views about the individual's right to privacy. (Funnily enough, the self-same, moralistic guy or gal will probably have no qualms over submitting the boss to such treatment – for one's seniors seem to be fair game when it comes to seeking skeletons in the closet. . . .) Lest you do feel a twinge of conscience in all this, let me hasten to add one important rider. The sole objective of my recommended prying on staff must be to assimilate information which will enable the manager to make decisions which, by taking *all* circumstances and influencing factors into account, will be as correct and effective as is humanly possible – especially where the process of delegation is concerned. It goes without saying that the information so surreptitiously gathered must never, ever be used for other purposes (like gossip?) – *and that it would be well-nigh catastrophic if subordinates became aware of their manager's Paul Pry activities.*

> 'Uh-huh, Clive – but you're still in cloud-cuckoo land. . . . I'm a manager, right? No, wait a minute, let me finish. . . . My job is to get results – and if I do as you advocate and spend half my time snooping on the staff, I'll get nowhere, fast. . . . For goodness sake, be practical. They're adult people doing an adult job, and if they don't come up to scratch – well, that's what I'm paid for, to sort 'em out. . . . Gee, the way you talk, anybody would think I was running a flaming clinic or something. . . .'
>
> (*Spirited outburst by a manager during a seminar – which, to be fair, was supported by a general growl of assent from several of the others present.*)

Well, I did start off with a storm warning, did I not? This type of reaction, which might well reflect your own views, reader, is totally natural and one which I respect – but (and at this point I don my mortar-board) it is ill-advised. . . . To understand why this is so, it is perhaps necessary to step aside from delegation for a moment and consider the work of two particularly with-it guys in the art of management, Dr Blake and Dr Mouton – to wit, their *Managerial Grid*.*

You will see from Figure 5 that the Managerial Grid is literally a chart, on which an individual manager's 'concern for people' and 'concern for work' can be assessed on a nine-point scale – and, by plotting on the grid the point where these two assessments meet, his 'managerial style' identified. . . . What's that?

---

* Drs R.R. Blake and J.S. Mouton, two American professors, have been widely acclaimed for their perceptive and wide-ranging management research. Their Managerial Grid, featured in Figure 5, first came ashore in the UK in 1965, and has since been put to very good use by many leading companies as part-and-parcel of their management development programmes. Take it from me, this is no pie-in-the-sky management gobbledegook, but first-class, practical stuff – well worth your very serious attention.

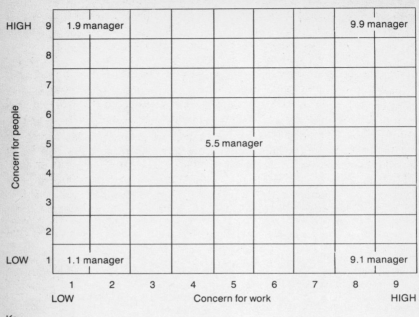

Key

1.9 manager	wholly 'people-orientated' – believes that only good, comfortable human relationships can make for efficiency
9.9 manager	believes that only totally committed people, working interdependently through a common stake in the organization, can produce results
5.5 manager	believes in an equal balance between 'people' and 'work' priorities
1.1 manager	the nil-effort, apathetic, son-of-a-gun 'manager'
9.1 manager	wholly 'work-orientated' – human relationships must not be permitted to interfere or hinder the organization task

Figure 5   *Managerial Grid*

'Here we go again – when is this crazy guy going to learn? Playing around with graphs, numbers and such-like. ... Yes, playing's the right word – I'm sorry to be rude, but you obviously don't have a clue about the realities of working life. ... D'you honestly believe that fooling about and giving people marks out of whatever for this'n'that 'style' is going to help me? Look, for the last time, I'm paid to run things and make a profit -and, goodness knows, that's hard enough these days, without all this nonsense. ...'

Right, have you done? Good, my friend, because if you had let me finish, I was going to say that it is not really the 'numbers game' that counts. In fact, you and I know that there are very few people, if any, qualified to assess accurately a schoolboy's composition on a nine-point scale, let alone set about rating a manager's 'style' and attitudes. . . . No, forget the business of actually arriving at a numerical assessment, *and regard the Managerial Grid for what it really is – yet another and very useful trigger for thought.*

Harking back to delegation and, for a moment, to the seminar chappie who objected so strongly to my recommended Paul Pry tactics, perhaps you can now guess the form of my response. . . . Aye, I introduced him in very general terms (and with the utmost tact, you understand) to the Managerial Grid. I invited him to plonk his digit on the *approximate* position which, in his view, reflected his people-cum-work orientation – and, after a few seconds' thought, he opted roughly for a 5.1 'work-orientated' point on the grid. (If I'm honest, I regarded him as a classic 9.1 horror, but it was neither the time nor the place for such arrant bluntness. Anyway, my snap judgement was probably way out.) But, certainly, in terms of this vital matter of 'people-orientation', he appeared to be a fairly hard nut, and I was not unduly surprised when his self-rating was later confirmed during a discussion with his boss – who confided that the man suffered quite some trouble with working relationships in general, and delegation in particular.

All of which, as per usual, prompts a question. . . . Using your overall reaction to the matter of eavesdropping on subordinates (and compiling what really amounts to mental or written dossiers on the good folk) as a handy basis for decision, where do you reckon *you* sit on the Managerial Grid? I am awake to the possibility that you may feel yourself so 'people-orientated' that the mere suggestion that you spy on your staff is unthinkable – and that nothing I can say will make you change your mind. If such is the case, it is a pity – but, far more important, and ignoring the Paul Pry theme, to what extent does your candid, albeit approximate, self-assessment reflect your approach to delegation? As I have said, forget all about numbers and grasp the big nettle – what is the trend of your managerial style, and how does this colour the manner in which you dish out tasks?

So much for keeping one's ear to the ground – except to add that, if the whole thing strikes you as absurd or morally unjustified, do have a serious rethink. . . . Let us now attempt to swallow what, to some, will be an equally bitter pill – the extent to which a manager's proficiency at controlling staff can make or mar his delegation skills.

Bash 'em, beat 'em – and hit 'em for six?

Umpteen millions of words have been written on the single question of how best to control one's subordinates, and I have no wish to bore you with yet more exhortations on 'being firm but kind' and all that jazz. Having thus

(I hope) defused any feelings of dread, I would like you to sit back comfortably in your chair and consider the following couple of quotes:

> 'As I've said, Mike's got his good points – but keeping a tight rein on his staff's not one of them. . . . I mean, he shouldn't have any trouble – after all, he's right in there with them, sitting in an open-plan office where he can see everything that goes on. . . . But it doesn't matter what time of the day I call in, it's always the same – people nattering away to each other like chickens in a hen-coop, wandering around all the time when they should be at their desks. . . . I tell you, sometimes it's absolute Bedlam in there – and what does Mike do about it? Not a thing. . . . In fact, what really annoys me is, I reckon he actually encourages them to behave as they do. I'm going to have to do something about it, or any hope of maintaining discipline is going to fly straight out of the window. . . .'
> (*Picture painted by Malcolm, the boss of a smallish but highly successful printing company, during the course of a general discussion.*)

> 'You know, I firmly believe that if you want to get the most out of any employees, and I mean ANY employees, they've got to be happy in what they do. By that, I don't mean dancing in the aisles or making the whole scene like an extended works outing – but, quite simply, that any manager worth his salt should do his utmost to create AND maintain a decent atmosphere, in which his staff can at least get some enjoyment from what they do. . . . I guess it means establishing – well, a kind of rapport with them.'
> (*Comments by a young manager during another such discussion.*)

What about the first quote? Having listened to Malcolm's comments on his office manager, I felt bound to ask the obvious question – what was the quality of work produced by Mike's team? Half-expecting to hear a tale of woe about slap-happy standards, failures to meet targets and so on, I was pleasantly surprised when Malcolm reminded me that he had kicked-off his grumble by saying, 'Mike's got his good points' – and then proceeded to tell me that he was unable to fault the work output from this avowed Bedlam of a workplace! Further discussion convinced me that, if there was a maggot in this particular apple, it certainly wasn't Mike – it was his boss who was at fault. While he had willingly moved to new premises, thereby putting his stamp of approval on an open-plan office layout, this did not mean that Malcolm, who was plainly a manager of the 'old school', had got himself tuned-in to modern outlooks and methods. His conception of office work retained a distinct flavour of quill pens and high-stools – and what he saw as the beginning of the end in the way things went on in Mike's domain was, in fact, the hallmark of an efficiently managed, highly participative and convivial work environment. I recall hoping for everyone's sake, and certainly for Mike's, that this otherwise charming old leopard would soon succeed in changing his spots. But I know I had my doubts.

As for the second quote – well, you have probably guessed that it was Mike giving voice to his own and, for my money, excellent point of view. It became clear in this second discussion that he was well aware of the older man's feelings in regard to discipline and, although he had great respect for

Malcolm, he was nevertheless determined not to change his management style just because his boss could not accept a more enlightened approach. At the time, I silently applauded Mike's strength of attitude, but not without a twinge of pessimism for his future. I remember asking myself, and I now ask you – how many managers, convinced in their hearts that they are right over something (and seeing this conviction amply confirmed by results), do stick by their guns in the face of the boss's disapproval?

But let us get back on course. . . .

HOW DO YOU RATE YOURSELF AS A CONTROLLER OF PEOPLE – AS A MANAGER?

No, do not attempt to answer such a blanket query right now. Instead, come up with some candid responses to the following questionnaire:

1   How would my boss (or, if I am lucky enough not to have a boss, one of my colleagues) describe my style of controlling people? I should do my level best to answer this question by dredging my memory for significant comments made by the person concerned – or by thinking about his or her revealed attitudes, which could tell all.

2   How would *I* describe my style of controlling people?

3   And, by further and frank resort to my memory cells, how would my subordinates describe my style?

4   Being utterly truthful with myself, do the *attitudes* displayed by these respective juniors bear out my response to the last question? I should remember that all-revealing factor, the look in a person's eye. . . .

5   Re-examining my answers to the first three questions and seeking out the variances which (provided I have thought deeply and well) I am almost bound to discover, which of these most accurately portray the truth?

6   Drawing the strings together and carrying out a mental re-assessment where my style of controlling people is concerned, what are my answers to the following, very pertinent questions?

   ●   To what extent is the 'projected image' seen by my juniors affected by my personal weaknesses of character, or whatever?

   ●   Truly, what are these weaknesses, and what am I doing to correct them – *really* doing?

   ●   Or am I going to take the easy way out, *once again*?

   ●   Enough of weaknesses, what are my personal strengths? Do I use these to the full when exerting my control over people?

   ●   Would my subordinates agree that the characteristics I have identified are, indeed, strengths – or would they deem them to be *weaknesses*? For example, suppose I identify one of my personal strengths as *'a pronounced ability to communicate with others'*, would it be the case, perchance, that my subordinates regard me (with far greater accuracy) as an over-talkative blow-hard – or as an overbearing, unfeeling dictator?

And now, just perhaps, you *are* in a position to answer that initial, blanket question: How do you rate yourself as a controller of people?

Keeping the motivation pot on the simmer

As an old, somewhat rogue-elephant college lecturer, I know it to be true that if almost any class-bound executive is asked to list the principle aims of management, you can bet your life that the word 'motivation' will figure prominently in the response. Sadly, I also know it to be true that, of all the manager-students who pronounce the term so trippingly on the tongue, precious few, however enthusiastic, actually *do* anything about motivating staff once they are back in their workplaces – or, for that matter, put to good effect much else of what they may have learned. Lest this sounds like a savage and unprovoked attack on all such folk, let me hasten to add there are two main reasons why these many good intentions so often go awry. Once back at the sharp end, their newly acquired knowledge and ideals are either engulfed in a tide of overwhelming apathy, or swept aside by a Force Ten gale of relentless bigotry:

'Well, Joan, that's your holiday over – now you'd better get down to work . . . .

'Yeah, that's all very interesting, but you just remember – this is where the action is, not the classroom. . . .'

'I don't care what the bloody textbook says – all that gubbins is strictly for the birds. You just get out there and do what you're paid to do. . . .'

'If I'd known you were going to come back full of nonsense like that, I wouldn't have allowed you to go to college in the first place. . . .'

'Look, m'lad, if you want to keep your job, remember this – here we do it my way. . . .'

If this is the type of thing that happens (and it is) to managers who have at least received some encouragement to act like managers, what are the chances for the legion of executives who have not received an ounce of formal training? The answer is self-evident – and if you want it spelled out, one could do worse than mention those five dreaded words, The Great British Management Disease.

So, here I am, yet another bright-eyed and bushy-tailed author, who knows full well that his particular cry –

EFFECTIVE DELEGATION DEPENDS ON A CONSTANTLY WELL-MOTIVATED STAFF

is destined at best to be merely one more voice in the wilderness. Or is it a simply marvellous case that you, my friend, know better? Has this sad-eyed evangelist for the cause actually found a kindred spirit in you – a manager who, come what may, will remain firmly motivated to motivate others? Hey, that's terrific – allow me to grab you by the ears and drag you through a few reminders of how to promote and maintain enthusiasm in your sub-ordinates. I use the term 'reminders' advisedly – because, remember, there is nothing new under this aeons-old management sun – depend on it, anything wearing a fresh label is just jargon.

Discussion   We have already dealt at some length with the need to encourage discussion where delegation itself is concerned, and I guess it would be an extremely thick-skinned person who failed to recognize that general discussion with one's staff, *when properly conducted*, is a very good method of enthusing them overall. But, assuming that you go along with this, do you make it a firm rule to hold such informal get-togethers on a regular basis? And,if so, do you take every care to obey the ground-rules for encouraging such debate? Do you:

- ensure that the sessions, as seen through the eyes of your sub-ordinates, remain discursive – and do not degenerate into command meetings?

- issue *all* those concerned with an advance note of some of the topics for discussion, and ask them to prepare their views and opinions? (No, *not* an agenda, merely some triggers.)

- when the discussions take place, remember to impose a polite gag on the garrulous, and actively (but gently) encourage the more reticent members to give voice?

- ensure (craftily) that the odd, quiet member of staff is seated nearest you, instead of being permitted to quietly merge into the background? This does not mean, of course, that you place such folk on the proverbial hot-seat, but merely in a position where, by dint of friendly prods, you can insure their active participation.

Suggestions   I would not be at all surprised if the merest thought of suggestion schemes sets your nerve-ends a'tingling. With the exception of a few, mostly richly endowed arrangements, they are largely unpopular with staff – and often regarded with suspicion by folk who have cause to doubt the underlying motives of management. But what about trying the equivalent of a *mandatory* suggestion scheme? The thinking executive who contrives to maintain an equable organization climate within his bailiwick will find it highly beneficial in terms of heightened morale and motivation to do just this. Simply get your thinking-cap on and, every so often, set this or that nominated individual a clearly defined and worthwhile problem area to tackle – something which is quite apart from his or her day-to-day work. It is, of course, absolutely essential that the outcome of this 'extra-mural' delegation is discussed at length with the person concerned, *and that any workable solution is placed into practice – preferably with its originator tasked with the monitoring of results.*

Management by objectives   This much-bandied technique is a further example of a topic which, if mentioned to the overworked 'average manager', is often received with more than a grain of exasperation. This is probably because the very term MBO smacks of a textbook, 'academic' approach to the intensely practical, day-to-day business of managing people – and is therefore construed as yet another attempt by the egg-heads to impose their Cloud-Cuckoo-Land influence. If this is your reaction, reader, please take another look.

The very essence of MBO is that instead of dictating to staff exactly how they should perform their work, they are given the freedom to strive towards clearly defined targets – and, thus, are left to work out their own salvation in their own way. The manager ensures that he is available at all times to give help and assistance – and conducts periodic, detailed reviews of progress and achievement in discussion with the people concerned, prior to setting new aims and objectives. In sum, MBO affords subordinates the opportunity to exercise personal initiative to the full, to accept responsibility and cope with challenge, and to have their performance regularly assessed and encouraged (which is a whole heap better than that frenetic business of the six-monthly or annual appraisal).

What it all boils down to is, there is no earthly use in trying to implement the 'motivation bit' in delegation if, as is so often the case, the overall state of staff morale (or whatever you want to call it) remains at a low ebb. Here is another prime area in which managers are supremely adept at deceiving themselves. . . .

> 'Well, you may have a point, Clive – but, speaking for myself, I've no real problems. . . . I don't regard myself as some sort of management saint, if y'know what I mean – but I'm quite confident that things are ticking over smoothly with my lot. . . . The climate, as you call it, is pleasant, and the work gets done – which must mean something. Quite honestly, I think you're overdoing this motivation thing – and, if you don't mind my saying so, getting a bit out of touch with reality. . . . We're not all idiots, y'know. . . .'

Hum, if that is your view, it could be that you are right – in which case, you will experience no qualms at all in addressing your thoughts to the following:

- On the basis of all the evidence available, is my interpretation of 'the way things are' shared by each and every one of my subordinates?

- What do I mean, *I don't know*? Is it truly a case that what they say and think when I'm not around is a closed book where I'm concerned? Are there really no clues?

- Keeping my eyes and ears wide open, what actually occurs when I casually enter their presence?

  a   Does their general conversation suffer a hiccup – and, if so, WHY?

  b   Does the atmosphere 'stiffen-up' or change in any way – and, if it does, WHY IS THIS?

  c   Do those who happen to be smiling suddenly change their outward mien – and if they do, WHY?

  d   When engaging in chit-chat with my staff, who invariably initiates it – them, or me? If I always seem to be the one who has to start the ball rolling, WHY IS THIS SO?

  e   Or is it the case that I seldom chit-chat with them – and, if so, WHY?

  f   When and if I move on, what do I think their reaction will be to my departure – TRULY?

And finally, if you wish to grapple with the sixty-four-thousand-dollar nub of motivation, take to heart one sterling definition of management:

> MANAGEMENT IS THE ART OF GETTING PEOPLE TO DO SOMETHING THEY DON'T WANT TO, AND MAKING THEM LIKE IT

Over to you!

Self-tutorial

First, a memory-prodder

Reconsider for a moment this business of learning all there is to know about your staff, and, in the same mental breath, think in terms of the *paternalistic*

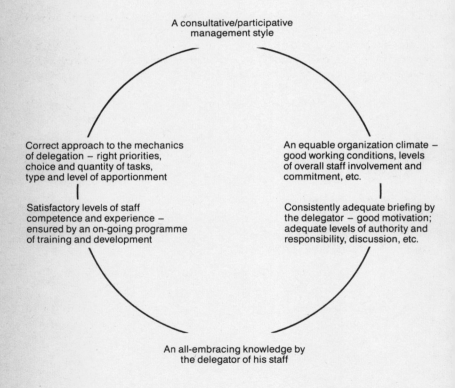

Figure 6   *An up-dating summary of the ingredients of delegation*

100

manager – the executive who believes among other things that he has a duty to concern himself with the overall physical and moral well-being of his subordinates at all times, in and out of work. If you accept my recommendation, and I hope you do, that you should become little short of an intelligence-gathering agency where your staff are concerned, it is necessary to remind you that one can retain the purest of motives – and then ruin it all by sliding headlong into paternalism. The discovery, say, that young Joe Bloggs is hiding an out-of-work skeleton in the closet, and that this could well be affecting some aspect of his performance (which, at best, is a somewhat dodgy assumption), may present an irresistible temptation to meddle. Plainly, this is a very grey area, bounded on the one side by the manager's unequivocal responsibility to interest himself in *serious* matters of staff welfare – and, on the other, by the Lorelei sirens of rank paternalism.

More drawing the strings together

Hark back to Figure 2 on page 68. We are now in a position to build on this diagrammatic summary of salient points in delegation.

Figure 6 might aptly be termed 'La Ronde' of the delegation process, but for one thing – we have yet to complete the circle. And that is exactly what we are going to do in the next chapter.

7 Well, boss, it's this way . . .

He stands, smiling encouragement, like a clumsy dentist.
Katherine Mansfield
The Garden Party, 'Bank Holiday'

I once had the misfortune to work for a boss who, possessing more than his fair share of virtues, allowed one of them to become an outstanding vice. Imbued with a rock-solid, overweening and totally undeserved confidence in his staff, this saintly individual was quite unable to conceive that his subordinates were other than perfect. As a consequence, any thought of checking on their performance or questioning their motives was viewed by him as totally abhorrent – and, I guess, as something akin to an unpardonable intrusion on their privacy. When it came to delegation, this implicit faith in the ability of his staff to do no wrong meant, quite simply, that he made no effort whatsoever to monitor progress or assess results – with the inevitable outcome that this thoroughly decent character was regarded by all and sundry as a nonentity, and someone to be pitied.

All right, 'Gentleman Jim', as he came to be called, was way out on the spectrum of management attitudes, and I have no doubt that you, reader, feel little pressing need to be reminded of the inviolable rule of delegation which, tragically, he ignored. But for all that, *and just in case*, here it is: *Never, ever forget to check on:*

> WORK IN PROGRESS
> *and*
> THE END RESULT

Let us grapple with these aspects, and see in practical terms if we can how the cookies crumble.

Coping with the running audit – and coping well

Assuming that we accept the importance of checking on the progress of delegated tasks, is it not making a mountain out of a molehill to go into further detail? One lass obviously thought so:

'I'm sorry, I don't mean to be rude, but – well, aren't you preaching the obvious? I mean, whenever I delegate anything, I always make a point of asking the person concerned how they're getting on with whatever it is. . . . I can't imagine there are many managers who don't do this – after all, what are we talking about? It's simply a question of asking, "How's it going, then?" or something like that – and if there are any snags, make no mistake, you get to hear about them!'

(Pauleen, a manager-student who, come rain or shine, ploughed her successful way through no less than four years of part-time college attendance, could always be relied upon for succinct comment during discussion – and the above was no exception.)

Point taken – and, ever so politely, rejected. . . . For the purposes of an effective running audit, it is *not* sufficient merely to pop one's head over a subordinate's shoulder at odd intervals and ask, 'How's it going, then?' Consider the risks inherent in such an approach:

- At the time of such 'casual' intervention, it could be the case that the person concerned is incurring a spot of difficulty, or hasn't even started the delegated task – and, contrary to Pauleen's view, is disinclined (for good or ill reasons) to let the manager in on the true state of play. In such cases the traditional rejoinder might well apply: 'Oh, er, fine, thanks. No sweat', when in fact the very reverse is true.

- If there is the slightest doubt in the subordinate's mind about the delegator's management style (and, whether one likes it or not, there usually is), even the most disarming 'How's it going, then?' will probably be construed along the lines that Big Brother is once again doing the rounds, and up to no good.

- Also and, sadly, not always in error, the subordinate may interpret the query as cogent evidence of the manager's lack of faith in his or her ability to complete the task without such intervention.

The secret of conducting a running audit (goodness, what is secret about it?) is to pre-empt such reactions by paving the way in advance. When delegating a task and once you have done your level best to obey the 'four-component rule', conclude the briefing with something along the following lines:

'Oh, and by the way, John, I'd be interested to know whether or not we're tackling this along the right lines – so, when you've reached the (so-and-so) stage, make a point of putting me in the picture, will you? Of course, in the meantime, let me know if you have any snags, and, together, we'll sort them out – but, otherwise, what about a brief natter on Monday morning? How does that suit you?'

The wise manager, who knows better than to trust to memory in such things, will make a note of the appointment – and the subordinate, now committed to reporting back on progress, will know exactly where he or she stands. Last but certainly not least, in thus arranging an interim discussion the delegator

APROPOS OF SOMETHING No. 11

Once upon a time I worked for a boss who really should have been a Centurion in the XVth Roman Legion. His only and very firm conception of auditing progress on delegated tasks was to parade all the subordinates *en masse* at a set time each week (t'was 09.30 every Monday morning), take advantage of his exceedingly large office by marching up and down the line of assembled troops – and then proceed to bark a standard litany of questions at each and every man-jack of 'em:

CENTURION: 'Right, Burroughs, your job was . . .?'

BURROUGHS: *(A mumbled response)*

CENTURION: 'I see. Progress . . .?'

BURROUGHS: *(More mumbling)*

CENTURION: 'Have you FINISHED it . . .?'

BURROUGHS: *(And more, punctuated with the odd stutter)*

CENTURION: 'WHY NOT . . .?'

And so on, down the line.

Funnily enough, he suffered from flat feet and goodness knows what-all, and had never served in the armed forces, so at least they were spared.

will have demonstrated more than a touch of discerning management style – and this can only be to the common good.

All of which, of course, can be ruined if the ensuing get-together is not conducted along effective and profitable lines. . . . Some managers, having successfully paved the way for a good feedback session, will still be tempted to trigger the thing off with those dreaded words, 'Well, how's it going, then?' – and, if they do so succumb, will be back to square one in a trice. There *are* better alternatives:

'Right, Joyce – perhaps you'd like to kick off by giving me a run-down on your progress thus far. . . .'

'To start with, Jim, I'd like you to put me in the picture – tell me what you've achieved. . . .'

'Knowing you as I do, Anne, I'm pretty certain you'll have made a sizeable dent in the job by now – fill me in with some details, will you?'

And so on.

The sole object of the exercise must be to provide the subordinate with an open-ended opportunity to recount progress, rather than what could well amount to a heaven-sent opportunity to take an easy escape route with such banalties as, 'Pretty well, thanks'. The running audit should also provide the subordinate with a further opportunity to chip-in with suggestions and opinions; for the point cannot be stressed too much – by and large, it is the person who does the work, not the delegator, who will encounter any difficulties and discover possible short-cuts. Lastly, some further encouragement will never go amiss, will it?

The importance of really assessing the end-product

Ask any delegator, 'Should you check on the outcome of completed tasks?' and precious few will reply in the negative. 'Oh, absolutely', or words to that effect, will be the common and emphatic response. It is therefore somewhat ironic that, when it comes to the crunch, this self-same majority of managers will so often prostitute their art, viz:

'Jean, have you finished all those estimates for Yates?'

'Oh, yes – they went off this morning. . . .'

'Good-oh!'

End of conversation . . .

It should be the aim of every manager to extract the maximum 'benefit' from any situation – and, in the case of checking the outcome of delegated tasks, this objective assumes quite massive importance. Only a properly conducted assessment will reveal *all* the crucial issues involved:

● Has the task been completed as required – and in its entirety?

● Does the outcome of the work satisfy the original requirement – or, for instance, has its performance uncovered factors which were previously unknown, or simply overlooked?

● Assuming that the work was correctly allocated (i.e. to the person(s) adequately qualified to carry it out), with what degree of proficiency has it been performed – and what needs to be done to correct any revealed shortcomings?

● Did the job provide a sufficient challenge to the person(s) concerned – and, if not, was the work wrongly allocated?

● Conversely and with the benefit of hindsight, was the task too difficult

APROPOS OF SOMETHING No. 12

The occasion, an in-company training session on delegation – the speaker, a young, newly appointed supervisor:

'Clive, I wonder if I could say something? (*Encouraging nod from yours truly.*) 'I don't want to tell tales out of school, but. . . .' (*More encouraging nods.*) 'Well, I've had one or two of these, what d'you call them, feedback discussions with my boss – and, having listened to what you and the others have said, I don't reckon they were much of a success. I shouldn't say this – I mean, you all know who I work for. . . .' (*This time, everyone present nods violently – and there are indications all round that the lass should ignore protocol and carry on regardless. Such is the reaction that, remembering the MD's expressed wish that everyone on the course should be urged to speak their mind without any qualms, I succumb to temptation and give the final nod.*)

'Well, anyway – take the last time it happened. . . . As usual, he was frightfully nervous and just couldn't look me in the face – in fact, he looked everywhere but at me, and this didn't help at all. . . . He started off by muttering something about hoping that I'd finished the mail-shot, because if it hadn't caught the afternoon mail he'd get it in the neck from upstairs. Apparently he'd promised Mr Teape that we'd have it all done by the weekend – but, of course, he hadn't told me that. As you can imagine, I was a bit upset about this. . . . I reminded him that he hadn't given me any definite deadline, that all he'd said was, "Get the job finished as soon as possible", and that was what we had done . . . .' (*Murmurs of 'Typical . . .' all round.*)

'Anyway, I went on to say that by the time we'd got the price lists printed-off, the afternoon mail had gone, and there wasn't a hope of us getting all the stuff enveloped-up and addressed before Monday. . . . Unless, of course, he'd authorise overtime that evening – when we could finish off, and I'd take everything to the post office on Saturday morning. Well, you all know what he's like. . . . At this, he started chewing away at his bottom lip, muttering that I'd let him down, or something like that – oh, yes, he said that it wasn't much good having me as a supervisor if I couldn't manage a simple thing like a mail-shot. I wasn't having that, and I told him so – I reminded him that if he wanted a job doing properly, it was up to him to make sure I was put in the picture in the first place. D'you know what he said?' (*A chorus of 'We can guess' replies from her colleagues.*)

'He said the idea of having me in for a discussion was to check how I'd done on this particular job – that he'd delegated an important task to me, and that I'd utterly failed him. . . . By this time I was really mad, and I was also dead-sick of the way he kept squirming around in his chair, refusing to even look at me – I honestly don't know how I stopped myself telling him what to do with the job! I ask you, what d'you do when you're saddled with a man like that?'

There were many suggestions from the assembled group, some of them quite rude. But the point is, this 'manager' continues to occupy his seat of power – as do thousands like him. How fortunate that such an approach to delegation is totally alien to *your* nature. . . .

- and, in this context, what can and should be done to prevent recurrences of such complications?

- If, during the briefing, it was agreed that the job should embrace some element or approach actually suggested by the subordinate(s), how did this contribution work out in practice – and what recognition-cum-praise is therefore due?

- What lessons in delegation have been learned for the future?

The pros and cons of the verdict

In reminding you yet again that managers are only human, after all, it is necessary that we also acknowledge the single most dangerous, endemic weakness to which *homo sapiens* is prey – namely, the unerring ability of John Doe to open his mouth and plonk his size-eleven foot straight therein. You will not need me to remind you that this proclivity for ill-considered tongue-wagging has been the trigger for centuries of human tragedy and disaster – and, so far as the world of management is concerned, has been and continues to be the root cause of far too many of its ills. If, perchance, there is a maxim which should be engraved on the heart of every executive, it surely must be that sterling admonition delivered to the Roman Emperor Augustus by the poet Horace:

'*Et semel emissum volat irrevocabile verbum.*'

(Once a word has been allowed to escape, it cannot be recalled.)

But that is not all. If we paused to think about this business of what we say, we would realize that our subordinates make a positive fetish of latching-on to even the most trivial of comments; weighing each word for its individual worth, assessing intent – and, above all, using their conclusions as a primary basis for a highly perceptive, on-going appraisal of the boss's prowess and expertise. Thus it is that the quality of a manager's reaction to the outcome of delegated work will not only have a profound effect on working relationships and staff morale in general, it will also do much to make or mar his reputation. Note that it is the *quality* of a manager's verbal reaction that counts; quite plainly, the choice of words will often constitute a well-deserved rocket – but, whatever the intent, the quality must shine through. Thinking in terms of *your* outcome-of-task discussions, pose yourself the very thorny question: if you were magically privy to your subordinates' thoughts (which, thank goodness, you are not), which of the following would you most wish to overhear?

'Gee, I've worked like stink on this damned job – and all I get in return is a blinking "Finished, eh? Good-oh!" brush-off.'

'I wonder if he could say "Thank you" without having a coronary?'

'Hey, it was decent of her to put it like that. . . . I'll say this of the boss, she certainly appreciates good work – not like that other so-and-so. . . .'

'I knew I'd get away with it! Pulling the wool over that guy's eyes is an absolute doddle. . . .'

'Bloody hell, that was some telling-off – but I'll give him his due, everything he said was fair enough. . . . From now on, I'd better watch my step.'

'How can anyone be so uninterested? Just wait until I tell the others about this . . . .'

'He really is a pig's orphan. . . . I don't know why he bothers to have staff – never listens to reason, just goes ranting on and bloody on. Old Bill's got the right idea – somehow or other, we'll just have to drop him in it, up to his scrawny neck. . . .'

'It's a pleasure working for old Diane. . . . She really knows how to say thank-you – AND mean it.'

'The trouble with him is, he just talks for the sake of talking. . . . I wonder if he's ever sincere?'

'He tries to let on that he's got the job taped – when, in fact, he knows damn-all. . . . One day he'll get the boot – and good riddance to him, that's what I say.'

'Poor sap, he really is a sad little character. . . .'

You are probably anticipating the question, but do you know the answer?

WHEN YOU DELIVER YOUR JUDGEMENT ON A COMPLETED TASK, WHAT DO YOUR SUBORDINATES THINK OF *YOU*?

What was that?

'I said, as a matter of fact, Clive, I couldn't care less what they think. It's about time you realized that a manager's paid to manage – not worry about what his staff think of him. I do my job as I see fit, and they haven't sacked me yet. . . . I'm getting just a wee bit sick of this mealy-mouthed nonsense – I thought you said you were going to offer practical advice?'

I must admit, reader, if such is your reaction, it is backed by a whole stack of precedent. .... Assuming that, like most managers, you are fired with an ambition to climb the promotion ladder, you will have craned your neck and looked up at the Elysian fields – and compared your own undoubted attributes with those of this and that top-rung incumbent. Ah, yes, and what do you see? That's right, umpteen 'captains of industry' who have got where they are today by the simple process of treating people like £-signs – who, although they may not care to admit it, are fervent believers in the Adam Smith philosophy of 'Treat 'em like machines for maximum return.' The thing is, this particular breed of leaders tend to stick out like the sore thumbs they truly are; attracting those (including you?) who believe that the only road to success is the one paved with other people's necks. The real captains of industry, the men and women who have earned their positions by dint of hard work and *caring* leadership, are not to be seen jostling for a place in the limelight. They feel no such compulsion, for they are not addicted to the heady scent of publicity – nor are they afflicted with an ulcer-making, utterly false sense of values. But, of course, if you have the authoritarian bug searing the walls of your veins, letting loose its venom on others as well as effectively shortening your life – well, you will dismiss this stuff as nonsense, and I must presume that you are prepared to pay the price.

Enough of all that. In the words of the poet, I intend to press on regardless!

Make praise work

The award of praise for a job well done should never, ever be considered as merely a managerial nicety – as a doggy biscuit or figurative pat on the head to mark Fido's latest achievement. While this is an important and underlying purpose, the true objective of praise is to fan that proverbial fire in the belly of the recipient – to the extent that he or she is stimulated to take on bigger and better things. It is in this context that the 'Oh, jolly good, you've done well' type of praise assumes quite banal proportions – for, if it achieves anything, it is usually limited to triggering a sense of pleasurable complacency in the person so addressed. A further disadvantage of such limited, blanket words is that they often convey to the subordinate a strong impression that the manager possesses only a very peripheral knowledge and appreciation of whatever has been achieved – and, correct or not, this will lead to a rapid lessening of respect for the boss.

With these points in mind, consider the following examples:

a   'Joe, I've had a good look at all that work you did on the Watchett account – and I must say, I'm very impressed. 'Twas a very good effort – keep it up!'

b   'Joe, I've had a good look at all that hard work you put into the Watchett account – and I must say, I'm very impressed. I particularly liked the way you tackled that business of his latest complaint. . . . He's an awkward customer, but you've obviously managed to placate him without involving us in remedial work, which really would have knocked our profit margin for six – very well done. Oh, yes, and I see you've sorted out the delivery dates for those wretched injectors – that must have taken some doing! Now, look – how d'you feel about doing a similar first-class job on the Baker account – it's a knotty old problem, but I'm more than confident you could give 'em a good run for their money. . . .'

True, example *b* would take very much longer to put across, but would it not be time well spent? The fact is, while Joe's initial feeling might well be 'clobbered again', it is likely that this almost reflex mental response will be swiftly supplanted by a desire to rise to the challenge. Lest you entertain doubts, remember that even the most skilled of delegators will never be able to prevent his subordinates grumbling about their lot, for that is the rock-solid privilege of any workforce, or manager. What matters is that, having traditionally vented their spleens, subordinates set about things with a will to succeed – and, for my money, example *b* is vastly superior to example *a*, in that it paves the way for just such as this.

Finally, is it necessary to remind you that praise is exactly like chilli sauce? Applied with the greatest of care, it will transform the flavour of staff motivation – but dollop it on like tomato ketchup, and, believe me, you'll never forget the experience.

And criticism, too . . .

Most of us have attended courses or meetings at which the resident Big White Chief has called for the members to voice 'constructive criticism' of this or that topic – and probably all of us would at least claim familiarity with the term. Why is it, then, that so many people, given the task of criticizing in constructive vein, kid themselves that they are proceeding to do just that by prefacing wholly *destructive* comment with transparent and enemy-making palliatives?

'Don't get me wrong, but. . . .'

'I mean this in the nicest way. . . .'

'I don't intend this to sound destructive, but. . . .'

'I know you won't mind my saying so, but. . . .'

'I'm sure you wish me to be frank. . . .'

I can guarantee one thing; unlike the mental myopia suffered by countless executives, subordinates can spot the warts on destructive criticism at a hundred paces – and, quite rightly, they swiftly come to detect those who, in their view, should know better. Consider, if you will, the following:

a 'Penny, I've read your copy on railway safety – and, well, I don't want to discourage you, but it's just not good enough. .... I mean, for a start, what on earth made you go for that style of lead-in? Talk about putting people off – why, if I was intending to go somewhere by rail and I happened to read that, I'd never go near a station again.... And look at the way you've described the Harrow and Wealdstone business – it reads like something out of a penny-dreadful. .... I know I told you not to pull any punches, but this is ridiculous – for goodness sake, take it away and come up with something I can use.'

b 'Sit yourself down, Penny. I'd like to discuss your piece on railway safety. I've read it through – and, well, there's no doubt that you've really gone to town on this one.... But before I wade in with my comments, I'd like you to fill me in on why you chose this particular approach – after all, it's pretty stern stuff, isn't it? ... 'Uh-huh, I see. ... Okay, you've certainly achieved that with your introduction. But, tell me, d'you not think it would be a good idea to preface the Harrow and Wealdstone bit with a para or two on the positive side? Say, something on overall safety statistics – which, let's face it, are pretty good....'.... Yes, I think it's on to highlight the odd disaster in the way you have – but I'd like you to use your inimitable style in presenting a more balanced view. Maybe you could be crafty and turn the stats to your own advantage – y'know what I mean. ... So many million passenger-miles per single fatality, which is terrific – unless you happen to be that one fatality.... It's an excellent piece, Penny – it just needs that final touch of yours to round it off. ...'

Once again, I think I heard the vestige of a rejoinder. ...

'Huh, if I went to those lengths, I might just as well have done the job myself – how much time d'you think I have in a day?'

I would like to think that such was not your reaction, reader – for, going straight out to the end of the proverbial limb, I am sure that you of all people recognize the salient need for constructive criticism. Don't you?

And, because it's sometimes necessary, admonition. . . .

Sadly, we do not ply our management wares in a perfect world. Just as our own ranks are salted with a hefty number of ill-performers, so indeed are those of our subordinates – and, every now and again, it falls to our individual lot to deliver an admonishment for work poorly done. However, before firing-off such minor or high-calibre rockets, it is absolutely essential that the delegator carries out a spot of candid introspection:

CAN I BE POSITIVE THAT THE POOR OUTCOME OF THIS TASK IS IN NO WAY DUE TO MY OWN SHORTCOMINGS?

- Did I delegate the job to the right person(s) – in terms of qualifications and experience?

- Was my briefing adequate in every respect?

- Did I allow sufficient time for successful completion of the job?

- Did I, albeit in innocence, interfere in any way while the job was being carried out, thus creating additional complications or undue pressure?

- Have I taken all mitigating circumstances fairly and squarely into account?

All of which, of course, is the cue for you, reader, to accuse me yet again of preaching the obvious – but before you do deliver your indictment, give a little thought to this question of admonishing poor performance. Imagine, for example, that young Charlie has just delivered the results of his (hopeful) labours for your scrutiny, and there it is, right before your eyes – solid evidence that in some respect or other he has fallen down on the job. Faced with such an everyday contingency, can you *honestly* say that you proceed through a searching questionnaire, as outlined above, and reach a *considered* conclusion before launching your rocket? Be a devil, and admit that there are times when we are so taken up by the disappointing outcome of a task, that the admonishment comes tumbling out without a vestige of such logical thought – which is why, if we are decent souls at heart, we sometimes feel traces of guilt when our employees, duly rocketed, have slunk out of our presence.

Continuing with the example and assuming that your delegation-conscience is thus clear, it is now necessary for you to consider (and I do mean *consider*) the type and form of your admonishment. While it is clearly beyond the purview of this book to take a detailed romp through the jungle of discipline at work, there are one or two points that are well worth mentioning – so let's mention them.

The dreaded attitude   Are you one of that army of managers who, when faced with the need to admonish or reprimand a member of staff, reaches down into your desk drawer for what I like to call the Actor-Manager's Disciplinary Po-Kit? See if you recognize the components. . . .

- *The Po-Set-Square*   A handy instrument for ensuring that, prior to the admonishment session taking place, the desk-top is impressively dressed for the great judicial occasion; all extraneous papers cleared away – with trays, blotter, pencils and what-not meticulously positioned with geometric precision.

- *The Po-Mask of Rectitude*   A perfectly fitting mask which, when slipped over the manager's face, converts his or her habitually pleasant features into the totally alien (and hence, somewhat comic) visage of the Lord High Executioner – all the better to pronounce sentence with. . . .

- *The Po-Style Fix* A do-it-yourself hypodermic injection, which produces an immediate straightening of the shoulders, a stiffly upright posture – and a strange effect on the user's larynx, ensuring that all utterances are delivered in coldly sepulchral, judicial tones . . . .

Well, do you happen to have a Disciplinary Po-Kit in your bottom desk drawer? If you do, be assured that your subordinates know all about it, and have many a scornful laugh at your expense.

Embarrassment-cum-awkwardness While you may not be addicted to the Po-Kit, it could well be the case that, like so many of us, you feel ill-at-ease during any session with staff which entails delivering a reproof. While this is entirely forgivable, it is wise to remember that *allowing such emotions to show* does nothing to help the proceedings or enhance your reputation. A few managers try to camouflage this weakness by resort to a deliberate overdose of sternness – which, of course, brings us straight back to the Po-Kit syndrome. A stern manner is very often essential, but an overdose is well-nigh suicidal.

Choice of words Remember what Horace wrote, and choose your words with deliberate care. Depend on it, to most individuals, a telling-off is a significant event, and certainly one in which a manager's words and *implications* will be committed very much to memory – for possible and effective later use.

It's good judgement that counts

Each and every post-delegation assessment of results should be conducted with two aims in mind; firstly and obviously, to complete an effective audit of what has transpired – and secondly, to make good future use of the information so gained. It is in this latter area that managers, especially those who are overworked and continually striving to meet various deadlines, tend to be dilatory. Time, the great enemy,* has to be treated with respect, but it is quite amazing how many of us refuse to spend some of this valuable commodity in planning for the future. We are so caught up with the hurly-burly of current demands and events that we fail to acknowledge that 'x'

---

* Depending, of course, on how we've got along together with all this stuff, you may care to note that another book of mine, *How You Can Do More in Less Time*, also published by Business Books, provides a battle-kit for the manager determined on victory.

time expended now can produce 'x + y' time saved next week, next year, or whenever. So, with that second aim of post-delegation assessment in mind, the truly effective executive will think along the following lines:

- Has the carrying-out of this task highlighted the need for innovation or change – the institution of new measures or procedures, the scrubbing of obsolescent ones, etc.? Or, perish the thought, if the completed job is of a recurring nature, is its continuance really necessary?

- How will revealed staff training needs be tackled – and who, for fully comprehensive effect, will be involved?

- What the devil *are* the personnel, administrative or organization lessons to be learned for the future?

- Last but not least, as the instigator of this piece of delegation, how does my overall performance rate – and what can I do to ensure that *I* am better in the future?

There is a fairly weighty self-tutorial coming up – but, having stuck with me thus far, I am conident that with the help of a goodly measure of your favourite tipple, you will win through. Get to it!

Self-tutorial

Exercise verdict

For this first exercise, imagine that your subordinate has greeted your arrival at the office with those hopeful words, 'I've finished that job you gave me,' and that, as a consequence, it is now time for you to implement the last, vital step in the delegation process – the assessment of the results. How, in terms of good management planning, will you carry this out? Jot down your step-by-step procedure – and, as usual, we will compare notes later on.

Exercise treat-her-right

Joanne, a bright and breezy member of your staff, has been with you for just over two years, during which time her overall performance has been consistently good. Liked and respected by her colleagues, she has become noted as a person who is ever willing (and generally able) to help any one of them in the minor work difficulties that sometimes occur. Her attitude is frank and forthright, and she displays a commendably responsible attitude to her job – while, at the same time, clearly expecting others to possess exactly similar attributes.

A week ago, when your department was working at maximum pressure, you found it necessary to burden Joanne with a particularly complicated piece of work – telling her that, although the task was somewhat outside the terms of her job, you thought it well within her capabilities to perform. She, in fact, was doubtful about this – but, after some persuasion, she agreed 'to have a jolly good try'.

Joanne has now completed the task, which entailed a considerable amount of paid overtime, and you have just finished going over the results. To your dismay and despite your most careful briefing, it is evident that she has made a series of compounding errors which mean that the job will have to be done all over again. You are certain that the lass is unaware of her failure – and, since she is clearly awaiting your comments, you know that you must have her in for a post-mortem within the next few minutes.

What, in essence, will you say to Joanne?

Another pause for thought

Call to mind a task which you have recently delegated to one of your subordinates – and, employing your accustomed self-candour, compare the manner in which you assessed the outcome with the step-by-step procedure in Figure 7.

So, how did that last assessment session *really* go? With hand on managerial heart, answer any of the following questions which cause you unease:

- If you praised your subordinate, can you be certain that your laudatory comments were not received with quiet cynicism – as further evidence of an insincere manager venting yet more of his hot air?

- If criticism was the order of the day, and even if you tried your hardest to make it constructive – can you be certain that the recipient would agree? Is there the faintest chance that your perceptive subordinates regard you as an expert in carping criticism?

- And if you opted for censure, how likely is it that the person concerned left Your Majesty's presence with the thought, 'Hey, that was one hell of a reprimand, but I deserved it – and, despite the fact I've just had my tabs torn off, I wouldn't work for anyone else'?

- Consider the question of revealed training needs. Are you one of those managers who blithely comes out with such comments as, 'Well, we'll have to ensure that you get some tuition in so-and-so' – and then proceeds to do absolutely nothing about it?

- Or do you habitually (or even occasionally) chuck such training needs to the four winds by the simple means of getting them 'to sit by Nellie'?

116

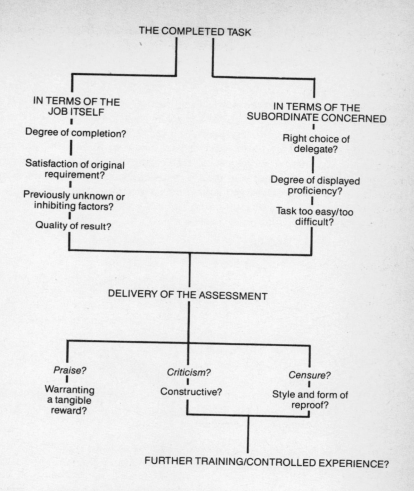

THE COMPLETED TASK

IN TERMS OF THE JOB ITSELF

Degree of completion?

Satisfaction of original requirement?

Previously unknown or inhibiting factors?

Quality of result?

IN TERMS OF THE SUBORDINATE CONCERNED

Right choice of delegate?

Degree of displayed proficiency?

Task too easy/too difficult?

DELIVERY OF THE ASSESSMENT

Praise?
Warranting a tangible reward?

Criticism?
Constructive?

Censure?
Style and form of reproof?

FURTHER TRAINING/CONTROLLED EXPERIENCE?

Figure 7   *The assessment of completed tasks*

● When you hold your post-task get-togethers, do you contrive, albeit unknowingly, to convert a so-called discussion into one of those wretched command sessions – with but one voice to be heard throughout the entire proceedings?

Notes on exercise verdict

Assuming that you did have a stab at this exercise (now there's an underhand imputation, if there ever was one), I'm sure you will have checked your jottings against the details in Figure 7 – and, just maybe, also discovered some relevance in the above questions. But, at the risk of flogging a willing horse, there is another aspect to be considered. . . .

While you may be entirely happy about the format and content of your post-delegation discussions, what about the actual time spent on these sterling events? While a thirty-second natter with a subordinate may be all that is required in respect of mundane work commitments, it will certainly not suffice as the final stamp on a job which has involved prolonged effort. Unfortunately, there are managers who utterly fail to equate the depth (and hence the quality) of their assessment discussions with the complexity of the tasks concerned – with the inevitable outcome that the poor old subordinates become rapidly disenchanted with their boss, and with work as a whole. So, when did you last pay attention to the question of *taking your time* over these more significant assessment chores?

Notes on exercise treat-her-right

A simple exercise with an all-too-obvious answer? Yes, I think few would deny that, if a manager did shovel out delegation in the manner described in this little account, he or she would be gambling (either knowingly or unknowingly) on the outcome. However, do not be inclined to dismiss the scenario lightly, for it highlights an almost endemic and very damaging management weakness: the tendency of many executives to allow the urgency of a task to override their common sense – and when this results in failure, to compound their sin by throwing completely undeserved blame on the subordinates concerned.

While you, reader, may have rightly opted for an 'admission of guilt' and even an apology to Joanne, the hard fact is that the real-life outcome often proceeds along very different lines:

> 'Look, Joanne, I'm not going to beat about the bush – I'm afraid you've fallen down badly on this one. . . . Despite the fact that I briefed you very carefully on what had to be done, you've made a number of extremely basic errors – and, well, this means there's simply no alternative, the whole damned job's got to be done all over again. Now, I know you weren't all that happy about taking it on in the first place, and I accept that you haven't had much experience on the contracts side – but, let's face it, a girl of your capability should be able to tackle this type of thing with her eyes shut. . . . To be honest, I'm very disappointed – and goodness only knows how I'm going to justify all the overtime you've knocked up, with nothing to show for it. What on earth got into you . . .?'

All right, perhaps you consider that the above 'quote' is painted larger than life – to which I can only reply, it is not. The all-consuming preoccupation of our Far Eastern cousins with never losing face is more than matched by the lengths to which a positive legion of so-called managers will go to escape an admission of culpability. It's called passing the buck. . . .

And now, *quo vadis*? Well, having given some attention to the matter of assessing individual delegated tasks on their completion, it is necessary to acknowledge that the periodic review of a subordinate's performance is largely concerned with how well the individual coped with a whole series of delegated jobs – so it's hey-ho for a grapple with formal appraisal. And that, as you must be aware, can be a right hornets' nest.

8 After the ball is over . . .

Marry, sir, they have committed false report; moreover, they have
spoken untruths; secondarily, they are slanders; sixth and lastly,
they have belied a lady; thirdly, they have verified unjust things;
and to conclude, they are lying knaves.

William Shakespeare
Much Ado About Nothing, Act V Scene i

In management circles at the sharp end, where the work *really* gets done,
one has only to mention the words 'staff appraisal' – and, wham, up goes the
proverbial balloon:

'Appraisal scheme? D'you mind, I've got more serious things to think about
. . . .'

'Look, friend, I don't need a piece of paper to tell me what to look for in people. . . .
I work with them, day in and day out – and, believe you me, I know what makes
them tick.'

'The only reason we've got an appraisal scheme is to keep those wallahs in head
office happy. It gives them yet another load of bumph to shuffle around. . . .'

'You know as well as I do – it's just a game to keep that shower in Personnel in
business.'

'Show me an appraisal scheme – and I'll show you trouble. . . .

For all the above cry-from-the-heart reasons and, because, like it or not, the
process of appraisal is indissolubly linked with the outcome of delegation,
we have to set the beast into some form of perspective – so, first, let's have a
good go at doing exactly that.

The entire business of appraisal is concerned with *evaluation.* If you think
about it, we all engage in the broad process of weighing up anyone who
happens to cross our path, and this most certainly includes that motley
bunch of people – good, bad and indifferent – who constitute our seniors,
peers and subordinates at work. But, of course, there is a world of difference
between this very animal, almost reflex action and the deliberate operation
by an employer of a formal appraisal scheme – and it is the latter process
which demands our consideration.

Take the everyday story of working folk. . . . The vast majority of
employees kick off with an appraisal through the very dodgy medium of the
so-called selection interview. From this highly subjective start, the poor

beggars travel through an employment life which is the continual cynosure of evaluation by everyone around and, if they are so fated, by the additional inspection lamp of a formal appraisal scheme. In the event that this is the case, those affected will be acutely aware (assuming, that is, they have anything of consequence between the ears) that the very question of their continued employment, let alone any prospects of promotion, will depend on a system which, even if superbly designed, is fraught with the frailties and vagaries of its human practitioners.

The ubiquitous Joe Soap, for example, will know that although appraisal of one person by another is as old as the hills, his particular manager appears to be very much like the rest; ill-equipped with any real knowledge of human characteristics and the problems encountered in assessing them – even if he is a keen-as-mustard appraiser, which is not on the cards. Being well and truly on the receiving end, Joe also knows that a poorly designed scheme (or, equally, *any* scheme which is poorly implemented) will seriously affect his morale, stifle any loyalty he may feel for his employer, and place the dank pall of gloom and despondency over many of his working relationships. Lastly, if he is truly perceptive, he will know that an employer's decision to implement an appraisal scheme often stems from that virulent bug, organization vanity – the feverish desire by the top brass to try almost anything to ensure that the outfit presents what they see as a vigorous, thrusting and thoroughly with-it image. Yuk.

So, to the manager who, rightly or wrongly, is saddled with carrying out a periodic formal appraisal of subordinates, getting the process into perspective entails the whole-hearted acceptance of some very basic but vital points:

a   the near-certainty that the appraisal scheme concerned suffers from in-built weaknesses and snags;

b   the dead-certainty that, being human, the appraiser is equipped to make little other than subjective judgements of performance –and wildly subjective judgements of personality;

c   the second dead-certainty that the only people really to suffer from the serious consequences of *a* and *b* are the subordinates themselves.

Exactly how good is your appraisal scheme?

If, as is fairly likely, your position in the hierarchy is such that you are sandwiched between the policy-makers and those who really matter, what can you do as a middle-man to ensure that your appraisal scheme is as near-effective as possible? Well, reader, if you are one of those managers who regularly claims, 'Look, I'm not responsible for making the system, I'm just paid to work it', you can make a very courageous decision – namely, to stop being such a namby-pamby, and to get in there and start asking questions. If, on the other hand, you make no such claims, and your position is that you are merely up to the ears in apathy – then, for goodness sake, drum up some energy before it is too late and, once again, start asking questions.

Ramming the point well and truly home, here is a selection of questions for starters:

1   To put you in the picture (and, just maybe, nudge the consciences of those on high), what actual steps have *already* been taken to improve and maintain the quality of the scheme and the appraisers?

2   If the answer to Question 1 is a simple 'nothing', why is this so? Is it not realized that all the authorities on appraisal schemes urge the maintenance of *continuous and effective audit* of both aspects?

3   Should not something be done to determine the *validity* of the appraisal scheme as:

    a   a means of improving performance on the job?

    b   a basis for promotions and transfers?

    c   a method of establishing training needs?

    d   a means of raising morale?

    e   a vehicle for the discovery of supervisory and/or management potential?

4   How do the scheme's 'items for appraisal' compare with the following list?

The old favourites

Quantity of work	Quality of work
Co-operativeness	Dependability
Job knowledge	Initiative

Other 'job-related' items

Punctuality	Health and safety habits
Attendance	Good housekeeping

Other 'characteristics of the individual'

Adaptability	Powers of judgement
Resourcefulness	Powers of leadership
Leadership potential	Intelligence
Enthusiasm	Attitude to seniors
Attitude to peers	Attitude to subordinates
Tact	Integrity
Loyalty	Neatness
Powers of verbal expression	Powers of written expression
Health	Potential for promotion
Personality	Conduct

In this context, does the scheme require overhaul? If so, should not expert (probably outside) assistance be sought?

5   Should not the appraisers be trained (or further trained) in the art of appraisal – and, again, should not expert assistance be sought for this very knotty task?

Go ahead, question the system – and rally the support of your colleagues in ensuring, by fair or foul means, that those long-suffering subordinates are given a fair crack of the whip.

Do you accept YOUR frailties as an appraiser?

It is one thing to read about human fallibilities in appraisal, but quite another to accept that they apply not only to others, but also to one's own, highly nurtured self. Why, reader, have *you* not spent all your years coming up against people of myriad variety – and, as an inevitable consequence of this experience, developed the now deeply ingrained habit of weighing them up? Naturally you have, but just because your appraisal of others has become a habitual practice does not detract one iota from a hard and undeniable fact; to wit, *that everything you see, hear, feel and sense in others is filtered through the screen of your own innate views and prejudices.* If this were not so, if our lumps of grey matter were capable of error-free, computer-like assessments of others – think on't, we would be perfect selectors. There would be no broken friendships, shattered love affairs, divorce suits – or, for that matter, subordinates found wanting in this or that ability or characteristic. Alas, neither you nor I can lay justifiable claim to such perfection, and while this may make for a fairly eventful existence, it does precious little for all those poor souls at work who squirm beneath our appraisal eye.

As if all that were not enough, there is the additional factor that, when it comes to this business of carrying out a formal appraisal, very few managers enjoy the process. Unfortunately, it not only involves some head-scratching and a deal of paperwork – it also subjects many executives to that deeply personal horror of horrors, eyeball-to-eyeball confrontation. If the appraisal scheme is of the 'open' variety, the multifarious ratings and pen-chewing narrative comments have to be justified in discussion with the person being appraised – and we all know what that can mean, don't we? Weaker-kneed managers will deliberately moderate their assessments (it's called 'going for the happy average', or, if you are one for jargon, committing the 'error of central tendency'), thereby obviating the need for such embarrassing justification. Conversely, the ill-performing manager with some strength of personality will back his ropey, written assessments with sheer discussion muscle-power, aimed at reducing the subordinate to abject submission to his views. If either cap fits, friend, it's about time you stopped wearing it!

Getting to grips with the appraisal form

As I have already implied, many appraisal forms constitute a two-edged sword, in that they require the completion of numerical or alphabetical ratings under a variety of headings, and some form of narrative comment, to boot. This, in fact, is a good feature, provided one remembers the golden rule – the narrative must justify the ratings, and vice versa. But let us take a closer look at both forms of assessment, for there are a number of hobgoblins to be vanquished if the overall appraisal is to be worth anything at all.

Numerical and alphabetical rating

- Going for the happy average

Despite the all-too-obvious dangers, some appraisal forms are still designed with 'odd-numbered' rating panels; e.g.

	Low					High			
Initiative	1	2	3	4	5	6	7	8	9
Dependability	1	2	3	4	5	6	7	8	9
Accuracy	1	2	3	4	5	6	7	8	9

This design failing presents a standing invitation for the appraiser to commit the error of central tendency –to check off 'average' on the scales because:

a   the rater has insufficient knowledge to express a more discriminating opinion; *and/or b*   the rater has a basic fear of going to extremes, especially if the assessments have to be justified at interview; *and/or*

c   ratings of 'average' will not injure the person concerned; *and/or*

d   by going for average assessments, the rater seeks to conceal his or her lack of knowledge of the person being appraised.

So, if your appraisal form contains this fault, perhaps you have a further and pertinent question to put to those in high places. . . . In the meantime, do not be tempted to rate 'average' for any of the above reasons.

●   *The dreaded 'halo effect'*

Another common error committed by raters is to allow one rated quality to influence and colour their judgement throughout the entire numerical/alphabetical assessment – or, just as bad, to make all their ratings conform to a kind of overall impression of the person under appraisal. Sometimes the former weakness is prompted by the rater's extreme assessment of a quality not even mentioned on the form – thus, Joe Manager's consuming regard for Mary's beautiful legs may well influence his judgement in other areas
. . . .

●   *Failure to achieve common standards*

If ever you are in a suitable training or instructional situation involving 'assessment', be brave – and, after the session, ask your audience to rate your presentation by means of a simple (and anonymous!) assessment panel; e.g.

	Low							High
Knowledge of subject	1	2	3	4	5	6	7	8
Powers of expression	1	2	3	4	5	6	7	8
Ability to inject humour	1	2	3	4	5	6	7	8

Once you have plucked up sufficient courage to collate the results, an obvious fact will emerge; the ratings from your audience (although hopefully on the good side) will tend to vary – often like the March winds. This problem of the application of differing standards by raters can drive a coach and horses through the validity of any appraisal scheme, and is one of the urgent reasons why adequate training should be given to all who are required to carry out formal staff assessment. Such training cannot remove the problem (after all, what is the precise difference, say, between ratings of 6 and 7 for 'Leadership'?), but it can set out to improve the situation. Be awake to the question of varying standards. . . .

8	7	6	5
A consistently outstanding organizer and planner	In many respects an outstanding organizer and planner	Always a very able organizer and planner	Generally an efficient organizer and planner

4	3	2	1
A satisfactory organizer	Does not always organize satisfactorily	An unsatisfactory organizer	Unable to think systematically; works in a consistently haphazard fashion

Figure 8   *An improved assessment chart for the ability to organize*

● *A way round the snags*

One method of reducing the intense subjectivity of numerical/alphabetical assessment is to supplement the scales with carefully descriptive words or phrases. Figure 8 shows an example.

If your organization's appraisal form lacks these useful 'triggers', perhaps you should be asking a further question. . . .

Narrative assessments and summaries

It will be obvious that the appraisal weaknesses already described apply equally to the knotty business of penning narrative assessments and summaries – but I am afraid that the situation is complicated even further. The task of putting into words supporting arguments for particular numerical or alphabetical ratings (for, remember, one method must *justify* the other) also relies on the appraiser's range of vocabulary – and, even more crucial, his intensely subjective appreciation and application of the words in that vocabulary. Consider the following comments, made by a group of manager-students when asked to assess the efficacy of a visiting speaker:

> 'An interesting speaker, albeit that he had a flat voice.' . . . 'A dull and boring speaker who nearly sent me to sleep.' . . . 'Humourless and uninteresting.' . . . 'A serious presentation by a man who knew his subject – well worth listening to.' . . . 'The college should have known better than to engage this speaker. I thought he was terrible.' . . . 'A bit boring.'

Apart from the lack of consensus, one has to question the value attached by the users to such phrases as 'dull and boring', 'a flat voice', 'a bit boring', and so on. And, of course, faced with such verbal divergence, a question must be posed –who is right?

When writing narrative comment in appraisal (and, for that matter, in almost any other field of writing), it is essential to ask oneself some pertinent questions:

- In general –

  Am I consistently striving for objectivity?

- In particular –

  Am I allowing prejudice or partiality to taint my comment?

  Will others interpret my words in (as nearly as possible) the way I intend them to be construed?

  Does that which I am writing convey the exact sense and import that I intend – or is amendment, qualification or further definition necessary?

Today's average manager (I've tried to avoid using that term, but at long last it has slipped out) – especially if one considers the junior echelons of the hierarchy – is required to do much less actual writing than the guys and very few gals who occupied the executive seats of power in bygone days. In a way this is fortunate, for one of the most common observations made by examiners in the various professional institutes is the general inability of managers in the field of written expression – and, quite rightly, they see this as a cause for concern. In this man's humble view, the advent of the automated office (and, heaven help us, the automated executive?) should never be accepted as an excuse for poor standards of writing. Needless to say, I do *not* mean by stating thus that every manager should be a cloned Charles Dickens. . . .

Back to the original theme – when appraising your subordinates, watch the quality and import of those written narratives.

Playing the appraisal game

The topic of whether or not formal appraisal schemes are worthwhile is one which can, and usually does, provoke a great deal of argument – and, in any event, is beyond the purview of this book. Suffice it to say, then, that for every protagonist of formal appraisal, there will be a goodly number of managers who are heartily opposed to the process. Unfortunately, and artfully ignoring the rights or wrongs of the issue, such opponents (and sundry other, weak-minded managers) frequently allow their attitude to colour their actual implementation of appraisals. In short, the whole business becomes something of a game or contest, to be completed as expediently as possible, and with scant attention to the rules. As I have stated before, the only people who suffer from such scallywag approaches are the people being appraised – whose working lives can be placed in very real jeopardy by the ill-considered and wildly inaccurate reports that result. *Measured by any standards, this rotten managerial failing is little short of criminal.*

Drawing the strings together

If the process of delegation is to be anywhere near effective, it must entail the assessment and discussion with subordinates of completed tasks. Delegation of a series of jobs to an individual over a length of time will plainly entail a number of such investigative events, and the sum of the information thus derived by the manager will provide an overall picture of the subordinate's performance during the given period – for use, if necessary, in formally appraising that very thing.

It goes without saying (but, as you will gather, I intend to say it, anyway) that the absence of a *formal* appraisal requirement can never absolve a manager from the responsibility of carrying out periodic, informal reviews of performance. If you agree with me on this salient point, you will probably also agree that nearly everything in this chapter is relevant to the informal appraisal scheme – substitute 'verbal' for 'written', and there you are. Appraisal, whether it be in written form or tripped lightly off the tongue, involves just those rules, snags and pitfalls that I have attempted to describe. So, there really is no excuse, is there?

Self-tutorial

Exercise critique

This little task is quite straightforward. Take a look at the following snippets of numerical and narrative assessment, and note down anything that strikes you as significant. . . . We can compare notes later on.

EXAMPLE 1

	Low	High
Application of technical knowledge		1 2 3 4 5 ⑥ 7 8
Application of technical skills		1 2 3 4 ⑤ 6 7 8

Having completed just under six months' service in his new post, Jones has demonstrated a commendable ability to come to grips with the technical aspects of the appointment. I am particularly impressed with the manner in which he tackled the difficult Saudi Arabian project, when he provided an excellent lesson in practical supervision to his party of fitters by 'rolling up his sleeves' and personally tackling a number of mechanical problems – without any detriment to his role as team leader.

EXAMPLE 2

	Low		High
Expression on paper	1 2 3 (4) 5 6 7 8		
Oral expression	1 2 3 (4) 5 6 7 8		

I rate Pamela's powers of written expression as average for her position. So far as oral expression is concerned, I consider her to be moderately proficient.

EXAMPLE 3

	Low		High
Acceptance of responsibility	1 2 3 4 5 (6) 7 8		
Management of staff	1 2 3 4 (5) 6 7 8		
Reliability under pressure	1 2 3 (4) 5 6 7 8		
Drive and determination	1 2 3 4 5 (6) 7 8		

While Robert needs further experience to consolidate his first management appointment, he has grasped his new responsibilities with enthusiasm – and is plainly determined not to let anything stand in the way of his progress. I consider him to possess considerable personal drive, and rate him accordingly.

EXAMPLE 4

	Low		High
Foresight	1 2 3 (4) 5 6 7 8		
Penetration	1 2 3 (4) 5 6 7 8		

Judy is inclined to handle problems only after they arise, and I am afraid that she seldom manages to afford them other than surface attention. For these reasons I am forced to rate her as 'low-average'.

EXAMPLE 5

	Low							High
Appearance and bearing	①	2	3	4	5	6	7	8

This supervisor has never impressed me as being other than slovenly and ill-kempt in appearance and bearing – to the extent that I often feel he is long overdue for a good bath.

A pause for thought

One aspect of appraisal that causes many managers to scratch their heads is the question of how best to determine exactly which digit or letter finally to 'ring'. It may be of help to remember that the vast majority of people are average in virtually everything, *and that an individual must always be appraised in relation to his or her peers*.

Given, say, a 'six-point scale', ('A' to 'F') what approximate proportion of the population merits a rating for each letter, respectively? Again, we'll compare notes later on.

Exercise design-clanger

It's quite simple. Cast your eyes over the following extract from, would you believe, a real-life appraisal form – and note down your comments.

MANNER AND APPEARANCE

	Low			High	
Gestures	1	2	3	4	5
Facial expressions	1	2	3	4	5
Speech	1	2	3	4	5
Features	1	2	3	4	5
Poise	1	2	3	4	5
Dress	1	2	3	4	5
Personal hygiene	1	2	3	4	5
Courtesy	1	2	3	4	5
Interest	1	2	3	4	5
Height	1	2	3	4	5
Weight	1	2	3	4	5
Stamina	1	2	3	4	5
Physical disabilities	1	2	3	4	5

The self-same, incredible form also contained the following items. Jot down your reactions:

	Low			High	
Inclined to bear grudges	1	2	3	4	5
Easily dissatisfied	1	2	3	4	5
Easily discouraged	1	2	3	4	5
Difficult adolescent history	1	2	3	4	5
Lonely, poorly balanced life	1	2	3	4	5

We'll compare notes in a little while.

Now, since this is the final self-tutorial, I am going to widen its scope. See how you make out with a *pot-pourri* of mini-tasks.

A further pause for thought

Take any two managers known to you and, as a preamble, compare and contrast their management styles. Having done this, sit back and consider as objectively as possible exactly how their individual styles affect their handling of the delegation process.

When you have completed your analyses, compare the results with a candid and similar appraisal of your own management style and approach to delegation. Who comes off best in terms of, firstly, efficient task completion, and secondly, the maintenance of good staff motivation and morale?

Assuming that you have been impartial with your own self-assessment and, being but human, you've owned up to some shortcomings – which of the personal weaknesses are most overdue for remedy? How will you set about this vital obligation to yourself, and others?

Exercise head-scratch

Consider the following extract from a manager-student's paper on 'Delegation'. To what extent do you agree with his expressed views?

'I think that one of the main causes of universally poor delegation in management is the fact that managers, prior to being promoted to positions where they are required to practise delegation, are not taught the art or encouraged to accept it as a primary feature of working life. By this, I do not only mean the failure of employers to train potential managers for promotion (although this is obviously an important factor, requiring serious attention), but also that, from childhood, we are force-fed with the belief that delegation is a bad thing. From the minute that a baby begins to crawl, it is urged to walk, talk and do things by itself, to not rely on others in fulfilling these activities. The child's education, from infant school to the sixth-form, even in these more enlightened times, is still largely directed at the achievement of learning through self-help.

I happen to believe that Freud was right; the life-style and habits (etc.) inculcated in young people during their formative years will influence and even dictate their attitudes in later life, and I am sure this is true of the common attitude (a form of in-built resistance) to delegation.

'For these reasons I think that the much-needed management training in delegation should take account of the deeply-held 'for survival, do-it-yourself' attitude which, in my view, most people possess.'

By now, your carefully jotted notes should be piling up – but never fear, just press on!

Exercise parrot-knowledge

Probably owing to my own in-built resistance to change, I believe that small doses of 'learning by rote' are by no means to be condemned – and, whether you like it or not, I'm now about to apply a very simple test of your ability in this die-hard method of assimilating knowledge.

Imagine you are at your place of work (I ask you to imagine it because I cannot believe you actually have the time, or the sheer audacity, to read this book during working hours. . . .) and assume that, just for once, you are required to delegate a certain task – not verbally, but *in writing*. Hum, yes – so, bearing in mind the principles involved, select a suitably complicated task, and do your stuff.

If, perchance, you happen to be one of the very small minority of managers who do little else but pen such pieces of delegation – then, no, you are not completely absolved from carrying out this exercise. For you, there is a short postponement and a slight change of task; in that I would like you to drag out from the files a selection of your orders-cum-instructions, and subject each and every one to an in-depth scrutiny. Having acquired a handful, how, in terms of what you have read, do they stand up to such inspection? If you find yourself defending your brand of approach, pose one further, introspective question – are you being totally candid?

A brave spot of research

Invite your subordinate(s) to complete the following self-questionnaire:

1   What important aspects of the work within your terms of reference can you use your own judgement on, and make your own decisions about?

2   How, in your view, could these existing responsibilities be widened or increased?

3   In tackling your job and gaining the general experience that must accrue, are there any tasks which, delegated to you or to others, would

benefit the work of the department and all concerned if they were reallocated, revised or even completely reorganized?

4   Are there any tasks delegated to you which you could perform to better all-round effect if you possessed certain additional and specific authority?

Whether or not you dish out this kind of questionnaire (in discussion or in writing) will, I offer, depend largely on your personal management style and the state of working relationships within your bailiwick. In the event that you'd never dream of doing any such thing, then I suggest that very reaction provides adequate food for thought. . . .

Notes on exercise critique

Once again, the primary object of this wee task was to set you thinking in general about appraisal ratings and narratives, and I hope it achieved this aim. That said, compare your notes with the following, and let's see how we make out.

Example 1   With the benefit of absolutely no background knowledge, I am going to plunge straight in at the deep end – and suggest that the vital 'cross-justification' between the numerical ratings and the narrative is conspicuous by its absence. Friend Jones is described as a guy who apparently displayed no supervisory reluctance in getting his hands dirty and applying the skills of his craft, yet he is only rated 5 ('high-average') for this item – and 6 for the application of technical knowledge. What has happened in the mind of the appraiser where that written bit 'commendable ability' is concerned – is this reflected in the ratings of 5 and 6? Note that we are not concerned with substituting any preferred ratings; to make such an attempt in an exercise like this would be ridiculous – we are merely pinpointing areas of weakness. If this was a real-life situation, we would be forced to ask the question – which is the more accurate, numerical ratings or narrative comment?

Example 2   In this example the appraiser has utterly failed to justify the ratings of 4 with adequate narrative comment. Instead of providing some compelling arguments in support of the ratings, the two sentences say virtually nothing of value. Laziness, or lack of knowledge?

Example 3   Hey-up, is it really likely that Robert, rated 6 for 'acceptance of responsibility' and 'drive and determination', merits a 4 for 'reliability under pressure' – and does the narrative provide the required justification? I'd say this is another potential case of doubt – which is the more accurate form of report, ratings or narrative?

Example 4   I'll polish this one off by offering that the reported inclination by Judy to handle problems only after they arise merits a rating of 1 or 2, not a 4.

And I reckon the same applies to that rather wonderful item, 'Concentration'. It's the same old question – which section is one to believe?

Example 5   Well, so far as the narrative goes, it could be said to go some way towards justifying the rating of 1 – but it doesn't go far enough. In such cases the appraiser must detail what action has been taken to correct the gross failing or weakness. In this example, such evidence as there is suggests that the appraiser has merely put up with the filthy rat-bag, if that is what he actually is. . . .

It is very much on the cards that you will have disagreed with at least some of the above comments. This, if anything, serves to confirm the intensely subjective nature of the appraisal round. I would only add that there is nothing like gnawing on a bone of contention to sharpen the wisdom teeth – and as you might well have gathered, that's exactly what I set out to do.

Notes on a pause for thought

Utilising that statistical wonder, the normal distribution curve, as a basis for coming up with some proportions, your figures should look something like this:

> 3 per cent of the population merit an A rating
> 13 per cent of the population merit a B rating
> 34 per cent of the population merit a C rating
> 34 per cent of the population merit a D rating
> 13 per cent of the population merit an E rating
> 3 per cent of the population merit an F rating

It is at this point that the 'pause for thought' is not only desirable, but very necessary. . . . Consider that relatively minute 3 per cent of the population who merit a superlative A rating – and, of course, the 3 per cent who, being beyond the pale in whatever quality or trait is under appraisal, merit a rating of F. The crux of the matter is this: before you dish out that A to Joe Bloggs, does he *really* qualify for branding with such a stamp of excellence? Conversely, does the assessed cretin of the outfit *really* deserve that horrible F award?

I make no apology for emphasizing this important point. If, for example, I am appraising my assistant accountant, can I honestly record that he possesses a personal characteristic or aspect of performance of such quality that, of all assistant accountants, my guy is better in this respect than *97 per cent* of 'em? The likelihood is, I can't – and, if you face the odds fairly and squarely, nor could you.

Notes on exercise design-clanger

As I mentioned earlier, I gleaned the items listed from an actual appraisal form – and, up to a few years ago, it was used regularly and terribly by a company of considerable repute. So, if it happens to ring a bell, you have my condolences for a very tricky past, appraisal-wise. . . . Let us deal with its sickening nitty-gritty.

Firstly, and as I'm sure you will have noted, the rating scale used by the designer breaks a cardinal rule by affording a middle-of-the-road assessment, positively inviting the appraiser to commit the error of central tendency – an invitation which many will find difficult to refuse.

Gestures and facial expressions   What is required of the appraiser? What in blazes do these items really *mean*? Is it intended that one should 'rate high' (or 'low') for, say, the right royal, two-fingered variety of gesture – and what does the owner of a massive, once-every-ten-seconds squint rate?

Features   Again, the mind boggles. Does the rater award a 5 for a full set, and perhaps a 2 if the poor old subject happens to lack an eye or a nose? Or is it the case that this infernal designer requires the rater to pick out and assess – well, what? Beauty? Blackheads?

Dress   My advanced middle-age (not old-age, you understand) could place me firmly on one side of the generation gap where standards of dress are concerned – and *if* it did, what are the chances of my fairly assessing a subject against this ridiculous, one-word item? Really, what is required?

Personal hygiene   A wash a day keeps the rater at bay. . . . Quite seriously, is this type of thing necessary in an appraisal form? If you do have a valid need to rate personal hygiene, it would be wise to ensure that the item provides a bit more guidance for the appraiser than does this example.

Interest   Interest in what? Had the item appeared under a 'job performance' heading, one might have a clue – but it's listed under 'manner and appearance' and I, for one, don't have a clue. . . .

Height, weight and stamina   These faintly mysterious items again give rise to some mighty conjecture. One of my sons is a member of that elite force, the City of London Police, and he certainly had to satisfy a minimum height requirement before acceptance – but since Carl or anyone else is hardly likely to shrink, even in the rain, why have such an item on a periodic appraisal form? All right, I guess there's some excuse for 'weight' – if, that is, the organization concerned is unable to countenance fat-dab employees for some reason or another. As for stamina, the same comment applies – but what does it have to do with 'manner and appearance'?

Physical disabilities   Even if it is considered necessary to have this item at all (which, on a periodic appraisal form, surely cannot be the case), to list it under 'manner and appearance' is crude and rankly insulting.

Now we come to the 'emotional stability' group of beasties. The overall deficiency in this section is, of course, the inability of any appraiser to do other than guess at the method of rating to be employed. Does an assessed inclination to bear grudges merit a high or a low rating, and so on? The designer of this form clearly gave no thought to the basic mechanics of his creation.

To cap it all, on what grounds is the run-of-the-mill rater expected to base his assessment of such things as a 'difficult adolescent history' and a 'lonely, poorly balanced life'? It is all very well to offer that the ratings will be supported by narrative – but, going back to square one, are such items really valid? Ah, well, remember what I said about the bone of contention. . . .

So, was this pause for thought worthwhile?

A brief comment on exercise head-scratch

In my view this manager-student may have a point. There is little doubt that the common management failure to delegate wisely and well often springs from quite deep-seated attitudes, and one such mental disincentive could well be a hangover from an individual's formative years. Whether or not you tend to agree is really academic – the big thing is, any effect has one or a number of causative factors, and it is a healthy and very necessary exercise to seek them out.

Turning in the best textbook tradition to a spot of revision, what are the causes of your delegation weaknesses? What are you doing to eradicate them – and when will your ever-perceptive ears, roaming the range of your subordinates' private chit-chats, pick up the only comment that matters?

> *'I tell you what, though – when it comes to delegation,*
> *our boss is the tops.'*

Good luck!

9 Savouring the pill

Every man has a question which terrifies him, and to the
avoidance of which he gives himself with an energy that helps
shape his life.

Richard G. Stern
Golk

Way back in the introduction to this book, you may recall that I referred to
that common reaction by so many managers when asked about their
attitude to delegation:

MANAGER   *(Adopts a wise-old-owl look)* 'Delegation, y'say? Oh, good
delegation is absolutely vital, old chap. ... After all, the
whole damn shooting-match depends on it, doesn't it? *(The
wise-old-owl look degenerates in a flash, to be replaced by pickled-
onion eyes)* 'Oh, yes, indeed. ...' *(Fades into silence)*

Well,congratulations! By sticking with me (very nearly) to the bitter end,
you've proved that you, at least, are made of better stuff. So, with that
encouraging thought in mind, I'm devoting this final chapter to a concise
summary of what we've tackled – plus, because you're obviously a keen
reader, one last quiz session. Let's both be gluttons for punishment. ...

A delegation summary

- Delegation is NOT a party-trick of management; it is the essential, life-
  blood process upon which any organization depends for its continued
  existence.

- It is the assignment of correct levels of authority and responsibility to a
  subordinate for the purpose of carrying out specified tasks.

- On the face of it, delegation would seem to be an easy way of reducing a
  manager's routine chores; but, sadly, a number of executives are
  constitutionally incapable of handing out work to subordinates – they
  under-delegate.

- Such under-delegation arises from a variety of management ills: plain
  and simple lethargy; concern for one's precious prestige; fear of being

superseded; an overweening lack of confidence in one's subordinates – or, last but not least, a consuming interest in doing the job all on one's own.

- As if that were not enough, some managers ply their sinful practices at the opposite end of the spectrum – and *over-delegate*. This most reprehensible weakness springs from inadequate knowledge-cum-experience of the job, downright laziness, lack of personal motivation – or, in more than a few cases, aspects of fear.

- To delegate without establishing *work priorities* will invite colossal waste of time and effort, to say nothing of staff frustration.

- In allocating *authority* and *responsibility*, it should be remembered that POWER and ACCOUNTABILITY are being handed out. As with all explosives, handle like eggs. . . .

- All too often, managers tackle the vital question of exactly *what* to delegate by indulging in a kind of 'eeny, meeny, miney, mo' exercise. Such miscreants need reminding of the golden rule: *delegation is the means by which one's most valuable asset, ONE'S STAFF, are exercised and developed to the sensible limits of individual capability and potential.* A continual, running audit of subordinates' skills and experience is of primary importance to the executive who wishes to succeed.

- A manager's *span of control* can affect the quality of his or her delegation, and a good many other things, to boot. It takes courage to place one's 'breadth of bailiwick' under the microscope, but it must be done.

- For success, the *act* of delegation should comprise a cunning ad-mix of four essential ingredients: the actual instructions for the task; the allocation of authority and responsibility; the motivation of the subordinate concerned – and an opportunity for consultation and suggestions. Inadequate attention to these salient points will ensure that the attempted delegation is little more than a management farce.

- Ultra-discreet awareness of what is going on, staff-wise, in and out of work, is one of the keys to perceptive management – and is essential where effective delegation is concerned. But, again, this business of keeping one's ear to the ground is distinctly akin to handling explosives . . . .

- There are *some* bosses who reckon that on-going, all-pervasive motivation of staff (by means of regular discussion and encouragement) is psychological clap-trap. *There are many others who never think about it at all.* In terms of decent management in general, let alone delegation, both breeds invite catastrophe.

- The delegation process *demands* a careful running audit of work-in-progress, and a comprehensive assessment of each and every result. Good encouragement, genuine praise, constructive criticism, fair admonition – these are the arbiters.

- If there is a formal appraisal scheme in operation, it behoves the manager to remember that he or she has been *delegated* to conduct the process effectively – *and for the ultimate benefit of the subordinates concerned*. Adequate discharge of this single and vital responsibiity could entail the exercise of considerable personal acumen – and courage.

So, there we are, virtually at the end of the road. But, as I intimated, let's go out in a blaze of glory with some final questions.

A quiz for the keen

1   In certain organizations, the delegation process is implemented in an 'upward' direction. Name one such type of organization and briefly describe the serious problem commonly associated with this form of delegation.

2   What in a nutshell is a 'democratic' style of management?

3   One factor which can adversely affect the efficiency and overall quality of a manager's delegation is his or her span of control. Why is this so?

4   Plainly, when a manager encounters problems in delegating tasks to subordinates, their solution becomes a matter of the utmost priority. At such times, by far the best approach is to employ the 'six-step' problem-solving process. List these steps.

5   In discussing with subordinates the outcome of delegated tasks, it is necessary, as in all discussion with staff, that a manager should derive maximum profit from the sessions by the use of 'open-ended' questions. Describe one simple method of ensuring that all questions are open-ended.

6   One root cause of over-delegation is, of course, a manager's inadequate knowledge and/or experience – and, in this sobering context, Dr Laurence J. Peter has provided a renowned and salutary warning to us all. What is it?

7   This inadequate knowledge/experience can embrace three specific areas. So, name them.

8   How may the phenomenon known as the Human Pecking Order adversely affect the delegation process?

9   What basic rules should be borne in mind when delegating authority and responsibility?

10   Name the five principle causes of under-delegation.

11   What are the two main points to be borne in mind when validating a task for delegation?

12   What are the likely perils of delegating inadequate responsibility for the performance of a given task?

13   Name the two factors which, in combination, can dictate the manner in which tasks are delegated.

14   Briefly describe the 'four-component rule' for the successful dishing-out of a delegated task.

15   Using the Managerial Grid as a basis for classification, an executive may be described as a '5.5 manager'. What, in essence, does this mean?

16   A very subjective question – but what can be said to constitute the interdependent, interrelated ingredients of effective delegation?

17   When assessing the outcome of a task, what are the three principal 'modes of approach' which can be employed in one's discussion with the subordinates concerned?

18   What style of management is best suited to maximizing the *all-round* benefits of delegation?

19   What is meant by the term 'halo effect' in staff appraisal?

20   When allocating responsibility for a delegated task, what should a manager never, ever do?

Answers-cum-crib-bank

1   Any organization in which the hoi-polloi, grass-root membership elects or, by other means, gains a leadership to which it delegates the job of representing the members' interests – a trade union, a professional association, a club, and so on. The potential and serious problem associated with such 'upward' delegation is that the leadership, once imbued with the heady scent of power, may partially (or utterly) abrogate their delegated responsibilities – which point reminds me that I should have included politicians in the above list. . . .

2   The 'democratic' manager will encourage his subordinates to discuss and debate anything of consequence – the big snag being that this pseudo-executive will also encourage them to make all the decisions. Motivation, control, discipline, and whatever 'from the top' will be

conspicuously absent – and 'the group' will have its corporate way in all things.

3   Because an excessively wide span of control (remember, the total number of people for whom a manager is *directly* responsible) will create difficulties in terms of delegation monitoring and audit – and almost everything else.

4   Identify the problem.
Gather all the relevant facts.
Establish the cause of the problem.
Search for and develop all the possible solutions.
Implement the most practical solution.
Evaluate the results.

5   By ensuring that all questions are prefaced with the 'magic six' openers, i.e.

What . . . ?   Why . . . ?   When . . . ?
Which . . . ?   Where . . . ?   How . . . ?

6   Ho, yes, the ubiquitous Peter Principle: 'In a hierarchy every employee tends to rise to his level of incompetence'. Lest you doubt this pearl of wisdom, look around you. . . .

7   Lack of *technical* knowledge/experience
Lack of *general management* knowledge/experience
Defects of personality – failure to put the knowledge over,
    inability to achieve general rapport, etc.

8   The 'institutional' pecking order (the levels of appointment in a hierarchy) and the 'human' pecking order (the natural dominance of stronger personalities over their lesser mortals) are not always one and the same thing within an organization. Hence, a strong-willed deputy may well dominate his or her nominated boss, to the detriment of the delegation process, *and* a whole heap of other things. Do you rule *your* roost?

9   *a*   Delegate only sufficient authority (power) to enable adequate performance of the task, never more.

    b   Allocate sufficient responsibility to make the delegate accountable for success or failure in carrying out the task.

10 Management lethargy, concern for prestige, fear of being superseded in the job, lack of faith in one's staff, and a consuming over-interest in the job.

11   *a*   Ensure that the activity concerned is one which should be delegated.

      b   Ensure that it is delegated to the member of staff most suited to carry it out.

12   Firstly and obviously, the subordinate's personal accountability for success or failure is almost certain to be severely eroded; secondly, such erosion may provoke skimping of the task – or even total neglect. An inevitable corollary is that the keen subordinate's motivation and general morale will suffer as a result.

13   The organization climate of the manager's bailiwick at the time in question, and his or her management style.

14   *Instructing* – detailing the task and giving the authority
Allocating – detailing accountability
Motivating – encouraging the subordinate's best effort
Consulting – seeking the subordinate's suggestions

15   A '5.5 manager' is an executive who believes in, and demonstrates, an equal 'concern for people' and 'concern for work priorities'. Where do *you* sit on the Managerial Grid?

16   A consultative/participative management style – a correct approach to the 'mechanics' of delegation – an equable organization climate – satisfactory levels of staff competence and experience – adequate briefing by the delegator – a sound knowledge by the delegator of his or her staff. . . .

17   *Praise* – and, in some cases, a more tangible reward
Criticism – ALWAYS constructive
Censure – choice of style and form of reproof

18   Whatever the autocratic monsters of the work-jungle may believe, only a consultative/participative management style can hope to maximize the all-round benefits of delegation. Naturally, you are well aware of this fact, but is your *alter ego*?

19   The weakness of allowing a highly rated quality to influence one's assessment of other, lesser qualities.

20   A manager should never, ever succumb to the temptation of plonking *ultimate* responsibility for a task on the hapless shoulders of a subordinate. None of us can hope to be saints, but committing this cardinal sin can send the offender straight to perdition – and it behoves us not to forget it.

Recommended reading

And here we face a wee bit of a difficulty – since, despite a fairly thorough search, all I can offer in the way of recommended reading are books which, albeit well worthwhile, have only a peripheral relevance to the process of delegation. If you come across a book dealing solely with the subject, please let me know – but if you happen to be writing one, don't bother. . . .

Berne, E., *Games People Play*, Penguin (1977)

Beveridge, W.E., *The Interview in Staff Appraisal*, Allen & Unwin (1975)

Biddle, D., and Evenden, R., *Human Aspects of Management*, IPM (1980)

Scott, J., and Rochester, A., *Effective Management Skills*, Sphere/BIM (1984)

Vroom, V.H., and Deci, E.L., *Management and Motivation*, Penguin Modern Management (1975)

Plus, for the real McKoy on your prowess in delegation – get your subordinates nine-parts-cut on their favourite tipple, and then pretend you're not listening.

Index